A HANDBOOK OF
PARISH WORSHIP

New edition

MOWBRAY PARISH HANDBOOKS

A Handbook for Churchwardens and Parochial Church Councillors — Kenneth Macmorran, E. Garth Moore and Timothy Briden

A Handbook for Council and Committee Members — Gordon W. Kuhrt

A Handbook for the Newly Ordained and Other Clergy — F. Vere Hodge

A Handbook of the Ministry — Wilfrid Browning

A Handbook of Parish Finance — Michael Perry and Phyllis Carter

A Handbook of Parish Music — Lionel Dakers

A Handbook of Parish Preaching — Gordon W. Ireson

A Handbook of Parish Property — Kenneth Elphinstone

A Handbook of Parish Stewardship — Gordon Strutt

A Handbook of Parish Work — Michael Hocking

A Handbook of Parish Youth Work — Clive Andrews

A Handbook of Pastoral Counselling — Peter G. Liddell

A Handbook of Pastoral Work — Michael Hocking

A Handbook of Sick Visiting — Norman Autton

A Handbook of

PARISH WORSHIP

(New edition)

by
MICHAEL PERRY
Archdeacon of Durham

and
CHRIS NEWLANDS
Precentor of Durham Cathedral

MOWBRAY

© Michael Charles Perry 1977, 1989
Christopher William Newlands 1989

ISBN 0-264-67175-9

First published in 1977.
New edition (entirely revised and reset) 1989,
Published by Mowbray, a Cassell imprint,
Artillery House, Artillery Row,
London, SW1P 1RT

Typeset by Acorn Bookwork, Salisbury, Wiltshire
Printed in Great Britain by Biddles Ltd., Guildford

British Library Cataloguing in Publication Data

Perry, Michael, *1933–*
  A Handbook of Parish Worship – New ed.
  1. Church of England. Public Worship
  I. Title   II. Newlands, Chris
  264′.03

  ISBN 0-264-67175-9

Contents

Introduction   *page* vii

1. The law of Anglican Worship   1

2. Laying the Foundations   11

3. Before We Begin   18

4. Morning and Evening Prayer   27

5. Holy Communion: Preliminaries   45

6. Holy Communion: the Service   59

7. Occasional Offices   80

8. Through the Year   102

9. Services for Special-interest Groups
   by Chris Newlands   111

10. Family Worship
    by Chris Newlands   119

Index   125

Introduction

I am glad that Mowbrays have asked me, after twelve years, to prepare this new edition of *A Handbook of Parish Worship*. The first edition was written in the mid-1970s, when the Church of England was still in the thick of liturgical revision and the Alternative Service Book was little more than a gleam in the eye of the chairman of the Liturgical Commission. Now we are in the late 1980s and The Alternative Service Book 1980 has been with us long enough for liturgical usage to have settled down and for observers of the scene to assess in practice its strengths and weaknesses. An archdeacon is well placed to be an 'observer of the scene'; the Canons lay on him the duty to 'bring to the bishop's attention what calls for correction or merits praise', and he can certainly see (and distinguish between) good and bad practice in the hundreds of churches to which he goes in the course of his duties. So I have kept my eyes open as I have gone around, and much of the advice in the following pages is the result of observing either dreadful or praiseworthy example.

The final two chapters of the original handbook have been replaced by material specially written for this edition by Chris Newlands, my next-door-neighbour and the Precentor of Durham Cathedral. A precentor has to meet all sorts of groups of people who wish to have a special, one-off, service, and he has to be sensitive to their needs and to know how it is liturgically possible to put their ideas into practice. Chris is good at doing that, and not only in the specialised setting of a Cathedral church, which is why I asked him to make his contribution to this handbook. Neither of us, however, should be held responsible for the opinions and idiosyncrasies of the other; what we have written, we have written independently.

Christian worship is the business of all God's people. The parson may be the professional, but he is only one side of the partnership and the other side of it is equally important. Parish worship must therefore be based on an understanding which is shared by both priest and people. To turn that principle from intention to reality, there needs to be in every parish a lively and informed group of lay people prepared to co-operate with the incumbent, to take trouble over the planning of the worship of the parish, to hammer out policies to present to the PCC, and to translate them into practice. This handbook is offered to the clergy and laity of the Church of England in the hope that it will help them to do so. There are, however, three things which it does not set out to do.

1. It does not aim to persuade parishes to adopt The Alternative Service Book 1980 as their sole liturgical fare. That book is an *alternative* to the Book of Common Prayer, the 1662 book which remains a liturgical standard for the Church of England, and the use of which is entrenched in English legislation. (From now on, we will use the abbreviations 'ASB' and 'BCP' or '1662' for the two books.) The liturgical ferment which began with the Parish Communion movement a generation or more ago and which reached its peak in the 1960s and 1970s, has led most congregations of the Church of England to use the ASB and to learn to value its provisions; but it would be a tragedy if the ASB were to drive the BCP entirely out of use. There are many churches where that has happened, and it has impoverished their worship. There ought to be room for both; a 'householder who can produce from his store both the new and the old' (Matt. 13.52) is better placed than one whose provisions are more limited. But the decision as to which forms of service to use, and on

which occasion, is a decision which should be made on better grounds than either innate conservatism on the one hand, or, on the other, the sheer desire to do the latest thing. The decision must be made carefully, prayerfully, thoughtfully, and for the proper reasons. Perhaps this book will help a parish to make its decisions.

2. This book is not concerned with the use of music in worship. Not because this is unimportant, but because it is *too* important and too wide-ranging to have anything but a whole volume to itself. Fortunately, it has one: *A Handbook of Parish Music* by Lionel Dakers (Mowbrays, revised edition, 1982), in the same series as this present volume.

3. Thirdly, we are not here concerned (except in the broadest way) with what the minister should wear during the service, or with liturgical choreography or ceremonial detail. Despite the disclaimer in Canon B 8 (5), which says that no particular doctrinal significance attaches to any particular form of vesture allowed under that legislation, the matter of what a clergyman wears and what he does during divine worship is still greatly determined by churchmanship, and we would not wish to enter into controversy in that area. This present volume aims merely to provide a broad basis of common ground, within which people of widely varying churchmanship may set their own particular ways of approaching the liturgy.

Positively, therefore, the hope is that the following pages should show what services are now authorised in the Church of England, indicate their broad characteristics, and give practical advice to the clergy, Readers, and congregations who want to know how to use them most effectively. It is a practical handbook rather than a book about the theology of worship. (I tried to deal with the theology in *The Paradox of Worship*, which SPCK published in 1977.)

Before we embark, a word to the clergyman, parish deacon, or Reader. You will be conducting public worship, and spiritually you will run the gauntlet of two possible dangers. At first, being new to the job, you will probably be so concerned with the mechanics of getting everything right that you will concentrate on the words and actions of the service and have no time left over in which to make the prayers your own. Don't worry; God understands. Pray as you prepare for the service, pray before you begin, and pray after you have completed it. Ask God to accept the sheer mechanical offering of the service itself as being the way in which you are trying to make it possible for other people to use it as the vehicle for their own prayers. Your own prayer lies in what you do rather than in the emotions that accompany it.

As you get more confident, so you will find it possible to pray at the same time as leading others in prayer. That is when the second danger, more insidious and more lasting, will begin. It is the danger of becoming so slick, so professionalised, and so used to a continuous round of services that what you do becomes automatic and prayer-less. Watch out for this, and if it happens, talk it over with a trusted spiritual counsellor. He will give you the right advice for your condition. Sometimes it will be that there is nothing to do but soldier on through a period of spiritual aridity until things come to life again, and meanwhile to be doubly careful to conduct the worship as carefully as possible so that the congregation will never know your lack of feelings. Sometimes the advice will be that all that is wanted is an awareness of what is happening, and a resolve to be vigilant. Occasionally it may be more serious, and call for more drastic measures.

Most of the time, though, if things go as they should, it is a privilege and a delight to lead God's people in God's praises, and the prayers of the person at the front can be in tune with the prayers of the congregation, to God's greater glory. When that happens, it can be a source of the deepest conceivable joy and satisfaction to you. May it be so!

Finally: the basic conviction underlying this whole book is that worship is of the utmost importance and that it should be worthily offered to the best of the ability both of conductor and of congregation. Anything less than the best of which we are capable is unworthy of the God whose honour we wish to set out in our worship and who enables and inspires us to offer what he has given us in the first place—ourselves, souls and bodies, all we have and all we are. That is why the detail (and much of this book is occupied in matters of small detail) is important. Cumulatively, small details add up. If they can add up to worship offered with dignity and in joy to him whose service is perfect freedom, they will have been worth the trouble.

MICHAEL PERRY

The College, Durham
1 May 1988

The Law of Anglican Worship

An opening chapter on *The Law of Anglican Worship* is bound to seem rather dehydrated, but it is as well to begin by seeing what the law requires of us, and what we are allowed to do. There are legal enactments which tell us who may draw up forms of service, which services have been authorised for use, which services are mandatory, who decides what form of service is to be used where there are alternative possibilities, and what happens if agreement cannot be reached between the parties concerned.

Those who wish to consult the exact terms of the legislation controlling Anglican worship should look at the Church of England (Worship and Doctrine) Measure 1974, and the Canons stemming from it (mainly to be found in Section B of *The Canons of the Church of England*, Church House Publishing, London), but for most practical purposes the booklet issued by the Standing Committee of the General Synod will give sufficient guidance. Entitled *Public Worship in the Church of England*, it is revised from time to time in the light of synodical decisions. The fifth edition (January 1986) is available from Church House Bookshop, Great Smith Street, London SW1P 3BN, price 25p.

The law covers services in church or in any building licensed by the bishop under seal for public worship according to the rites and ceremonies of the Church of England. School services, therefore, or services in hospitals or other institutions are not included (unless the chapel is used and has been consecrated or is so licensed); nor are acts of worship in private premises. Every member of the clergy of the Church of England, before entering into office, has to declare that in public prayer and administration of the sacraments, (s)he will use only the forms of service which are authorised or allowed by Canon.

Who may draw up forms of service?

1. The General Synod may approve, amend, continue, or discontinue forms of service for use in the Church of England, subject to the following provisos:

(a) The proposals must have the support in Synod of a majority of not less than two-thirds of those present and voting in each of the three Houses (i.e. of Bishops, Clergy, and Laity).

(b) Any form of service approved must be neither contrary to, nor indicative of any departure from, the doctrine of the Church of England in any essential matter.

(c) The forms of service in BCP must continue to be available.

Any minister has discretion to make or use variations in these services, provided that they are not of substantial importance, that they are reverent and seemly, and that they do not depart from the doctrine of the Church of England in any essential matter. In the case of any doubt or question, the bishop of the diocese has to rule as to the interpretation of the phrases 'not of substantial importance' and 'in any essential matter'.

2. Where neither the BCP nor General Synod has provided a form of service, forms may be approved for use in a province by the Convocation or archbishop, or in a

diocese by the Ordinary (in most cases, the diocesan bishop). Again, they must be reverent, seemly, and doctrinally sound, and individual ministers are at liberty to make minor amendments.

3. On occasions for which no provision has been made by the Synod or other provincial or diocesan authority, the minister is at liberty to use services of his own devising. The same rules about reverence, seemliness, and sound doctrine continue to apply.

What services have been authorised for use?

1. The Book of Common Prayer of 1662 remains permanently authorised and could only be dislodged from its position by special Act of Parliament. The shortened forms of Morning and Evening Prayer from it as set out in the schedule to the Act of Uniformity Amendment Act 1872 (commonly called the 'Shortened Services Act') are similarly lawful, as is the service authorised by Royal Warrant for 6 February, being the anniversary of the Queen's accession.

2. The Alternative Service Book 1980 is authorised by General Synod for use until 31 December 2000, as are the services in the booklet ASB 70, which contains forms of service for use with the sick. Of the various services which appeared between 1965 and 1980, the only ones for which authorisation continues (until 31 December 1990, unless Synod extends the time limit) are Series 1 Marriage and Burial services, and Series 2 Baptism and Confirmation; but the House of Bishops declared on 26 January 1988 that the 'continued use, where well established, of any form of service which has, at any time since 1965, been canonically authorised', even though its authorisation may now have been withdrawn or allowed to lapse, remains lawful as not being of 'substantial importance' under Canon B 5 (4). Note that this allows any parish still using any Series 1, 2, or 3 service to continue using it, but it does

not allow a parish to introduce anew a service for which
general authorisation no longer exists.

3. The Archbishops of Canterbury and York have
authorised, without time limit, for use in their respective
provinces, a form of service for Remembrance Sunday.

4. Material authorised by the Ordinary differs so much
from diocese to diocese that it is neither possible nor
useful to detail it. It includes such items as diocesan forms
of service for the institution (or collation) and induction of
a new incumbent or the licensing of a person to a cure of
souls within the diocese. Some dioceses also have their
own forms of service for such occasions as the dedication
or consecration of churches or burial grounds, the opening
of church schools, and sundry other special occasions.

5. Where no other authorised provision has been
made, as we stated above, the minister may compile his
own services or use forms of service otherwise available.
Services for Lent, Holy Week, and Easter, and services of
prayer and dedication after civil marriage, have been
provided by the Liturgical Commission, approved by the
General Synod, and commended for use by the House of
Bishops. In some dioceses, the diocesan bishop as Ordinary has authorised them for use in his diocese. Where this
has not happened, the local parish priest has discretion to
use them or not, as he wishes, with or without amendment. The same applies to such matters as Sunday School
worship, family services which are not Eucharistic nor
derived from the BCP or ASB Daily Offices, services at
missions or evangelistic occasions, healing services,
'prayer and praise', or the worship of any particular group
which has asked for the use of the church for its devotions.
In all these cases, whether the forms of service are provided by the organisation concerned or not, whether they
are altered or not, whether the incumbent is or is not
himself conducting that service, he must remember that
the responsibility for the use of that form of service in his
church is his alone and it is his duty to judge whether the

material proposed is orthodox and suitable. The priest himself, or any member of the public, can appeal to the bishop for a ruling in doubtful cases.

What services are mandatory?

1. **The Holy Communion**. This must be celebrated in every parish church at least on all Sundays and principal Feast Days, and on Ash Wednesday (Canon B 14; the principal weekday Feast Days as listed in Canon B 6 are Christmas Day, Epiphany, Lady Day, Ascension Day, and All Saints' Day). In the case of any church which is not a parish church or of any other building licensed for public worship, the bishop may (Canon B 11 A) direct what services shall be held and what shall not be required to be held. Subject to this proviso, and subject also to the direction of the Ordinary, the Holy Communion shall be celebrated in non-parish churches as regularly and frequently as may be convenient (Canon B 14).

The requirement that the Holy Communion should be celebrated every Sunday in the parish church may be waived for some reasonable cause approved by the bishop of the diocese. A cause may be some long-term state of affairs (as, for example, when the daughter church is at the centre of population and the parish church virtually deserted) or something much more limited and temporary, such as during repairs or redecoration, or when the incumbent is ill or on holiday and no priest can be found to do his Sunday duty.

When the parish church is out of commission for a short time, and there is no other consecrated or licensed building in the parish, it is necessary to ask the bishop's permission to hold the statutory services elsewhere (Canon B 40). If it is to be out of use for a longer time, he should be asked to license the alternative building for a stated period. In some dioceses, the bishop will not grant his licence until the building has been inspected and approved by the Rural Dean (or even by the Diocesan Advisory Committee for the Care of Churches). Marriages cannot be solemnised according to the rites of the Church of England unless the building in which the service is to take place is a parish church or has been licensed for that purpose or unless the parties have obtained a Special Licence from the Registrar of the Archbishop of Canterbury. A building licensed by the bishop for Holy Communion is not necessarily licensed for marriages. In cases of doubt, consult the diocesan registrar.

The Holy Communion may only be celebrated in a consecrated or licensed building, except that the bishop may give his permission for it to be celebrated in any other suitable place, such as a private house or school or hospital. No such permission need be sought for the communion of the sick at home (Canon B 40).

2. **Morning and Evening Prayer**. These services must be said or sung in every parish church at least on all Sundays, other principal Feast Days, Ash Wednesday, and Good Friday. In churches which are not parish churches, the bishop may direct what services shall be held and what shall not be required to be held (Canons B 11 and B 11 A).

The bishop has power to dispense from the necessity of reading Morning and/or Evening Prayer in the parish church on Sundays, either on specific occasions or over a period. This often happens: the Parish Eucharist can make Mattins redundant, or the congregation at Evensong can become so sparse that priest and people decide it is no longer worth continuing. If the dispensation is to involve the discontinuation of either Morning or Evening Prayer for a period of more than three months the bishop is under obligation, before granting it, to consult either with the whole PCC or two of its members nominated by the PCC for that purpose. He may not use his powers under this Canon (B 11) so as to cause any church to cease altogether to be used for public worship. In this connection, 'parish church' includes a parish centre of worship so designated under the Pastoral Measure 1983 (Canon B 11A).

Every priest having a cure of souls is required to see that Morning and Evening Prayer are said daily, and the Litany on the appointed days, in one or other of the churches of which he is minister (Canon C 24). The minister of the parish, and all the other ministers licensed to serve in it, shall resort to church morning and evening to say or sing the Common Prayers and (on the appointed days) the Litany. The church bell is to be tolled beforehand to warn the people (Canon B 11). These requirements may be waived when the minister is not at home or when he is 'otherwise reasonably hindered', and he does not need to consult anybody else for dispensation. Reasonable hindrance ought certainly to include the 'day off' each week.

3. **Sermons**. Every priest having a cure of souls must preach in his church once a Sunday at least, or see that some other person preaches there, unless for some reasonable cause approved by the bishop of the diocese (Canon C 24).

Who decides what service is to be used?

1. **Morning and Evening Prayer and the Holy Communion**. The choice as to which of the authorised forms of service are to be used in the parish shall be made by the incumbent and PCC jointly. Note, however, that:

(a) They do not have to decide that one form shall be used throughout the whole parish and at all services. They could (for example) quite legitimately provide that the BCP should be used at some services or on some Sundays or in some of the churches of the parish, and the ASB at others; or that Rite A should be used on Sundays and Rite B on weekdays. They could, if they wished, decide on an experimental period during which a service is given a 'trial run', and take their definitive decision later.

(b) The laws of the Medes and Persians do not operate in this matter. A PCC may change its mind as often as it wishes. In practice it would not be wise to subject the parish to frequent fits of the liturgical fidgets, but there is nothing but common sense to prevent them from doing so if they feel they must.

(c) The decision relates to the service as a whole, not to options and alternatives within it. The law says (for example) that it is for the incumbent and PCC jointly to decide to use Rite A, but after that it is for the incumbent alone to decide whether to have the penitential section at the beginning of the service or later in the rite, or which of the four Eucharistic prayers to use: and any person officiating in the parish has to follow the instructions of the incumbent in such matters. In practice, of course, it would be advisable for an incumbent to have wide consultations with his PCC and congregation before deciding how to use a particular rite, and for them to come to a common mind on the matter.

(d) What about alterations to the text which are 'not of substantial importance'? Many members of the clergy, for instance, wish that the ASB had eliminated 'sexist' language, and they make sure that rites used in their own parishes are suitably doctored. They are at liberty to do so, but they should bear in mind that members of their congregation will worship elsewhere (on holiday, or at deanery or diocesan occasions). Alterations to the words spoken by the clergy may be accepted by a congregation as being idiosyncratic to 'their vicar', but alterations to the congregational parts will cause difficulty when the church is hosting a wider-than-parochial service, or members of the congregation are worshipping elsewhere. And, in any case, please, in your non-sexist emendations of the rite, try to avoid what *My Fair Lady* calls 'the cold-blooded murder of the English tongue'.

2. **Confirmation**. This is the bishop's service and the choice is his alone.

3. **Other occasional offices**. The minister is not legally bound to consult the PCC before deciding which of the alternative services to use. Any of the persons concerned in the ministration of an occasional office has the right to object to the minister's choice at any time prior to the moment the service begins. There is no legal ruling to define who is covered by the phrase 'any of the persons concerned'. Common sense would refer it to the parents and godparents at a baptism, the couple to be married in the case of a wedding, and the chief mourners at a funeral. Wider definitions could be troublesome.

What happens if agreement cannot be reached?

1. **Morning and Evening Prayer and the Holy Communion**. If there is deadlock between incumbent and PCC, until they can reach mutual agreement, the BCP forms must be used, unless other authorised forms had been in regular use in that church for at least two of the preceding four years (not necessarily on Sundays, not necessarily during the *last* two years, and not necessarily in one continuous period of two years). In that case, the PCC has the right to resolve that those alternative forms shall be used; but if the PCC will *not* so resolve, the incumbent does not have the same right, and 1662 is the only solution. But long before the sledgehammer of the law is applied in such a case, there ought to be a serious attempt to resolve the situation by bringing the disagreeing parties together under neutral chairmanship. The Rural Dean or lay chairman of the Deanery Synod, the archdeacon or suffragan bishop, or (in the last resort) the diocesan bishop could well be called in to act as moderator.

2. **Occasional offices**. If any of the persons concerned objects beforehand to the minister's choice of service and the minister is not willing to meet that request, the matter has to be referred to the bishop of the diocese for his decision, which is final.

So much for the law. Within its provisions, let us now see how the incumbent and PCC may best co-operate in planning the worship of the parish.

2

Laying the Foundations

In the short run, it is easier for the parish priest to be the liturgical dictator, benevolently controlling everything as though he believed he were the only person in the parish who knew what was really good for it. Partnership is harder work. It calls for teaching, prayer, care, and tact. But in the end it is the only worthwhile way of ordering the worship of the parish.

(a) It is correct legally. The Worship and Doctrine Measure insists that the choice between alternative services is the joint responsibility of priest and PCC.

(b) It is right pastorally and psychologically. When a congregation have been involved in the understanding and planning of parish worship, it can begin to come alive for them as *their* worship, and not as some externally-imposed clerical fad.

(c) It is also sound theology. Worship is an activity of the Body of Christ, and the local manifestation of that One Body is the unity of pastor and congregation. If worship both expresses and creates Christian fellowship, then the ordering of it is the business, not of the priest alone, but of the whole People of God.

The parson therefore ought to work with his people so that they can be at one in their liturgical understanding, their liturgical wishes, and their liturgical planning.

11

This is a long-term programme. It is not good enough to put a new service-book into the hands of PCC members and ask them to vote at their next meeting on its possible introduction into the parish. Those who are to make decisions about the worship of the parish need to have a background of awareness which is not achieved overnight. These decisions have, in the end, to be reached by the PCC as the representatives of the parish, but it is well to involve the whole parish as far as possible (not the PCC alone) in the educative and decision-making process. The question of worship could be a major item in the parish programme of lay training, and sermons, courses, parish conferences, weekends, and discussion groups could be related to it (though beware of over-kill!). Michael Hocking's *Handbook of Parish Work* (Mowbrays, revised edition, 1984) has a chapter entitled 'Parish Communication' which discusses these methods.

The understanding of the parish will ideally pass through three phases if services are to be ordered by priest and people together with an intelligent appreciation of what is being done and why. Let us, then, consider them.

Preparing with the PCC and congregation

1. **The nature and purpose of worship**. The basic groundwork is partly historical and partly theological. A congregation which is liturgically aware will know that Christians in different countries and different centuries have worshipped in different ways, that the rite with which it is most familiar has a long pre-history behind it, and that it was itself once thought offensively new-fangled. The congregation ought also to know what has been happening to the liturgy in the Church at large (and particularly in its own communion) during the ferment of the last quarter century, and how it has come about that they are using the rite they do. To achieve this measure of awareness in the congregation, the person who leads the parish study will find a great deal of help in G. J. Cuming's

A History of Anglican Liturgy (Macmillan, 1969), which takes the story as far as 'Series 1', and in *A Companion to the Alternative Service Book* by R. C. D. Jasper and Paul E. Bradshaw (SPCK, 1986).

This historical background, however, is of less importance than the theological understanding of what is happening when Christians worship. Here, the leader may like to consult Michael Perry's *The Paradox of Worship* (SPCK, 1977) and Michael Perham's *Liturgy Pastoral and Parochial* (SPCK, 1984). One aspect of worship is that it is the offering of its service to God by a particular group of people in a particular place and time, and it should therefore be set forth in a mode which honestly expresses the way they feel about God and the things they think it is proper to say and do in his presence. Worship must be grounded in a concrete situation; it cannot be planned in a vacuum. The right service for a particular congregation is one which best expresses Christian truth in the idiom natural to that congregation.

The purpose of worship is not primarily to educate or to evangelise. It is no good putting on a new rite because the incumbent thinks it would do the congregation good to be jolted out of their conservatism; nor is it any use for a staid congregation of elderly worshippers to put on services full of gimmickry in order, as the saying goes, 'to bring in the young people'. Folk see through that kind of disingenuousness remarkably quickly; mutton is no less tough for being dressed as lamb. Liturgical changes may *follow* changes in the composition and outlook of a congregation; it is disastrous to try and make them the *cause* of a changed outlook. The incumbent who forces Rite A through his PCC against the strong opposition of the 1662–minded congregation will find that the new service kills the congregation as quickly as they kill it. It is much more satisfactory to experiment within a framework of 1662 in such a case, and only to suggest a move to a new rite when the congregation is more flexibly-minded.

There are wrong and right reasons for wanting change. Wrong reasons are that everybody is doing it, or that 1662 is old-fashioned, or that change will attract newcomers. Right reasons for change are that the congregation have thought through their pattern and forms of worship and are dissatisfied because their present provision does not fit their actual situation. The purpose of this preliminary period of theological reflection is to establish an understanding of what worship is about and a realisation that if change is desirable, it is also possible.

2. **Worship in the parish**. The next stage is to look at the congregations in the parish and ask what pattern of worship would be most appropriate for them. Every parish is unique, so all we can do here is to suggest some of the questions which might be asked. For instance:

At what times on a Sunday do people want to come together for worship? What times are impossible (and why?) for what categories of people? What is the effect of TV programming on afternoon and evening worship? Are some times more suitable for older folk and others easier for young families with children? Is it right to expect the whole church to assemble at one single Sunday service, or is it better to have things fragmented?

What should be the relationship between Eucharistic and non-Eucharistic services? What is the relation between the Sunday School or children's instruction and the morning worship? By and large, our pattern is to have the children at their separate instruction until half-way through the Eucharist and then for them to join the adults. In some American Churches there has been experiment with a programme involving a Eucharist without sermon, with all the family present, after which the adults and the children separate to their individual groups and classes for the rest of the morning. Would that work in your parish?

Should baptisms normally take place in the afternoons and only exceptionally at morning service, or the other way round? (Don't forget that Canon B 21 directs that baptism should, unless necessity so require, normally be administered on Sunday at public worship.)

Is it necessary or desirable to have the same pattern every Sunday, or should there be a monthly rota of services rather than a weekly one? The scarcity of priests may necessitate a monthly rota, but its complications may put off members of the congregation who can never remember which services take place at which centre of worship on which Sunday.

How often ought the Eucharist to be celebrated during the week, and at what times? What times are best for the daily Offices—can there be times when some lay people can have the chance of saying their prayers with their parson?

Only when questions like this have been explored do we come to the detailed discussion of which rite to use and how to choose between possible alternatives.

3. **The choice of services**. There will probably be several distinct congregations in the parish, and they may well need different approaches. A parish norm is not necessary, nor is it always desirable, and the clergyman must be prepared to be flexible by using different rites at different times and places if both BCP and ASB are to have their proper place within the overall parish pattern, and if that is the way the congregations in his parish can best worship. The weekday Offices will probably be largely clerical rather than lay devotions, so that there the clergy may rightly expect freedom to innovate and experiment, whereas the early morning Sunday congregation are often more conservative in their tastes than that at the mid-morning Parish Eucharist. Services designed for the more elderly ought to keep to more familiar words and forms wherever possible. It was a retired clergyman who said to the author after a 1662 sick communion, a day or two before his death, that 'the old words are very comfortable'.

The later chapters of this book may help towards a

decision as to which alternative service to adopt. It cannot be emphasised too strongly, however, that no rite can be adequately judged by sitting down silently and reading it, or even by reading *about* it. One needs to know what it will sound like and what it will look like. If it is a service with a musical setting, there is that aspect to consider—with the help of *A Handbook of Parish Music* by Lionel Dakers (Mowbrays, revised edition, 1982). At the very least, there should be a public 'reading' of the service and some discussion of the different ways of presenting it. I would plead for more. The priest and a commentator should stage at least a couple of 'dummy runs' in church—one with the parish meeting and one with the PCC—before asking the PCC for permission to try the new service out for an experimental period of *at least* three months. It takes time for any congregation to pray their way into a new liturgy, and anything less than three months is totally inadequate for deciding whether a new rite is likely to be able to express Christian worship in a way acceptable to the congregation. After such an initial trial, it is fair to decide whether or not to continue. Without it, the case for change will in effect have gone by default.

The ASB services contain many permissible alternatives. During the initial period of trial, it is not wise to make too many unnecessary alterations. At a later stage, the changes can be rung to preserve freshness; at first, there is quite as much freshness in the unfamiliar rite as the congregation can cope with, and the need is for as much stability within it as possible.

As will be pointed out in later chapters, 'stage management' is important. At the Eucharist it has for some time been fashionable to take the Ministry of the Word from the reading-desk and lectern, the intercessions from the nave, and the Ministry of the Sacrament with the celebrant facing the people across the table. This certainly emphasises the structure of the rite and it is true that the newer liturgies in particular seem to go better if the celebrant faces West rather than East: but it is not a practice to insist upon in doctrinaire fashion. In some churches it is geographically possible. In others—particularly in those with cramped sanctuaries—it is not. In most dioceses, the DAC (Diocesan Advisory Committee for the Care of Churches) will be glad to talk about proposals for the re-ordering of worship with the incumbent and representatives of the congregation, and to arrange a site visit for a general discussion of what is possible and desirable not only liturgically but also aesthetically and architecturally. If the proposals involve moving the church furnishings or changing the internal appearance and arrangement of chancel or church (unless for a limited period by way of experiment) they must be authorised by faculty and the DAC must make its comments to the Chancellor. (For faculty procedure, see Chapter 3 of *A Handbook for Churchwardens and Parochial Church Councillors* by K. M. Macmorran, K. J. T. Elphinstone, E. G. Moore, and T. Briden, Mowbrays, new edition, 1987).

Keeping worship under review

Once a parish has a pattern of worship which has been evolved through mutual discussion amongst congregation, PCC, and incumbent, it is wise not to let the new arrangements harden and ossify. The PCC will probably find it useful to have a regular 'spot' on its agenda—perhaps annually, perhaps more often—at which any member may raise any question he likes, whether of detail or of broad policy, about the services and the way in which they are conducted. This kind of regular review of liturgical matters ought to prevent the parish from getting too inflexibly set in its liturgical ways.

3

Before We Begin

In some churches there is a worshipful and expectant feel to the place in the minutes before the service begins. In others, this is entirely absent. What can be done, before ever the first word of the service is uttered, to give an air of reverent and seemly devotion?

In the church

The church building itself will be clean and tidy. It will look as though people take seriously what the place is used for. The pews will be dusted, the floors clean, no piles of scruffy disused hymn-books or prayer-books, the sanctuary neat and its linen clean and ironed. The flowers will be fresh. If the building looks as though it inspires devoted care, there is better chance that it will draw out the best from the worshippers in it. If it is slovenly, then the service starts off in an atmosphere of 'anything goes'.

By the time the worshippers begin to arrive, the jobs of preparation will be over. Noise, rush, and fuss are incompatible with a calm ambience of peace and expectancy. There will not be a flurry of choir boys sorting out their books, the organist having last-minute consultations with the choir members in full view of the congregation, or the parson fretting around seeing that everything is in order. That will have been completed so that stillness reigns for at least the five minutes before the service begins. The organist will see to it that this stillness is helped rather than hindered by the choice of music and the way in which it is played.

If this is to be achieved, it is useful for the minister to have a check-list of duties and to arrange with the appropriate persons detailed to be responsible for them, that necessary things are done by an agreed number of minutes before the service. It might contain such items as:

Opening the church building

Choir books in stalls

Choir books in vestry for procession

Processional cross in vestry

Congregation's books ready for handing out

Places found in lectern bible

Necessary books in clergy stall

Credence

Altar books and vessels

Candles

Font ewer (if there is to be a baptism)

Hymnboards

Collection plate

Wine, water, wafers for offertory procession.

Opinions vary as to whether the congregation should be discouraged from talking in the pews before the service. To chatter could be thought irreverent; not to speak, to be unfriendly. If the geography allows it, the best solution would be to encourage chatter in the vestibule but to try and discourage it in the church itself. A great deal can be done by the example set by clergy, sidesmen, and choir before the service. Even so slight a matter as the choice of footwear can help—have your shoes rubber-heeled to prevent the noisy clatter that hard heels can make on tiled floors.

Candles are normally lit for the Eucharist and Evensong but not for Mattins. It is a matter of choice at the Eucharist whether to have the vessels made up and on the table under burse and veil before the service begins, or whether to bring them in at the entrance of the ministers, or whether to have them on the credence, not the holy table, and only move them into position when the ministry of the Word is about to give place to the ministry of the Sacrament. The author's preference would be to bring the vessels in five minutes before the service begins, and to have a server light the candles three or four minutes later. If the officiant is so in control of the preparations that he finds it possible to spend the time between the placing of the vessels and the lighting of the candles at the altar rail in private prayer, this will be found helpful to him in approaching the service in the right frame of mind—and it will remind the congregation of the seriousness of what they are about to engage in.

In the vestry

If the goings-on in the vestry can be heard in the body of the church, it is especially necessary to keep the vestry atmosphere calm and quiet. Even if it is right out of earshot, it is still important to remember that the choir, as much as the officiant and congregation, is taking part in an act of worship for which they too need to be spiritually prepared. Ideally, the choir should have a rule of reasonable quiet up to five minutes before the service begins, and should refrain from talking thereafter. Robing should be completed by two minutes before, and those who arrive later should expect to have to take their places in the congregation rather than with the choir. There are few things more destructive of choir reverence than the boy who arrives just as the procession is about to set off, and who has to be helped into his robes and have his hair brushed and the books thrust into his hands whilst the organist plays the opening phrase of the first hymn; but this phenomenon is far too frequent.

In some choirs, the robed section processes in, whilst the unrobed members do not do so. In that case, the unrobed members should all take their places in the choir stalls at the same time, and not drift in individually.

It may help to calm things if the choir is in its processional order a minute before time, with the opening hymn already found. The officiant then says 'Let us pray' and follows this with some such phrase as Ps 46.10—'Be still, and know that the LORD is God'. There can then be silence for some seconds, after which the vestry prayer is said, and the service is ready to begin.

Processions

Strictly speaking, a 'procession' begins at the high altar, goes round the church, makes one or more stops or 'stations' at particular places, and finishes at the place where it began. Such a procession will take place normally at the end of a service on a special feast day, and a hymn or hymns will be sung whilst it is in progress. Less technically, people commonly speak of a 'procession' when they mean the entry or exit of the clergy and choir at any service, and it is in this sense that the word is being used in this section.

The congregation stand when the choir and ministers enter or leave. The entry can be done in silence, or to music, or under cover of a hymn. Silence can be impressive, provided it is not too long. On the whole, music is better; it covers the incidental sounds and imposes less strain on choir and congregation. Hymn-singing is not to be commended. Hymns are items in themselves and should not be treated simply as covers for other activity. Get the choir in first, to give them their proper dignity, and to set the stage for the opening of worship: then have the hymn (if there is to be one) and give *it* its proper dignity.

The choir is often led by a cross-bearer, who waits at the sanctuary steps until everyone is in position before putting the cross in its place. If so, he moves away *before* the sanctuary party arrives, otherwise they have to push past him. If there is a verger in the procession, his position is immediately behind the choir and leading the clergy. Alternatively, the churchwardens, bearing their staves of office, can lead the clergy, then return to their places afterwards. If the bishop is present, a verger can lead the clergy whilst the wardens attend on the bishop. They sometimes do this for other diocesan dignitaries, which is flattering but (strictly speaking) incorrect. Although they are admitted to office each year by the archdeacon or his deputy, the churchwardens are the bishop's officers.

The speed of a procession, and the distance between the people who make it up, are matters which depend on the size of the church and the width of its aisle. Processions which go too slowly are more irritating than reverent (the same is true of hymns). The right balance needs to be drawn between rush and torpor. A procession ought not to be too closely bunched, but in a small church the distance between individuals cannot be very great unless the whole procession is to look silly. Only trial and error can solve this.

Reverencing the altar often causes processions to bunch up on the way in or straggle on the way out. It is preferable to have the whole choir facing east on filing into its stall, then to make a reverence together when the last member is in position; the whole choir then turns inwards together. Similarly, on the way out, the whole choir turns east together, reverences the altar, and is then able to file out evenly behind the cross-bearer.

Notices

At Holy Communion in the BCP rite, notices are to be given out immediately after the Creed, though there are other places at which they are appropriate. At Morning or Evening Prayer, if they are to be given out during the service, they should come immediately after the Grace and before the hymn, *not* immediately after the Third Collect.

These traditional places are no longer universally observed, and in many churches the notices are given out either right at the beginning or at the very end. Neither is without its difficulties. At the end they destroy the chance (which some worshippers rightly value) of a few meditative moments before returning to the secular world. At the beginning they will be missed by latecomers. If it can be done, best to have the notices duplicated, so that the officiant need only draw the congregation's attention to particularly important items, or (at the Holy Communion) to those specially relevant to the intercessions which are to follow. That prevents the notices taking longer to deliver than the sermon, which is not unknown. Written notices are, in any case, far more effective and easy to remember than spoken ones.

If they have to be spoken, remember that it is helpful to give the occasion first (thus alerting those members of the congregation to whom the notice is relevant) followed by the day and time.

For banns of marriage, see pages 88–9 below.

Registers

Canons F 11 and F 12 provide that the following register books shall be kept:

1. In all churches and chapels: a register book of services in which shall be recorded every service of public worship, together with the names of the officiating minister and (if he is a different person) the preacher; the number of communicants; the amount of the alms or other collections; and 'if desired, notes of significant events'.

2. In every parish church: a register book of baptisms. When a person is baptised elsewhere in the parish (for example, in hospital) the person performing the rite has to send a certificate in standard form to the incumbent 'as soon as possible thereafter' and the incumbent has to enter the baptism in the parish register with the words 'According to the certificate of . . . received by me on the . . . day of . . .' (Parochial Registers and Records Measure 1978, Section 2). Even if the hospital has its own register of baptisms, this procedure must still be followed.

3. In every church where confirmations take place: a register book of confirmations.

4. In every parish church or church licensed for marriages: register books of banns and of marriages. The latter has to be kept in duplicate and treated according to the regulations of the Registrar-General.

5. In every church having a churchyard open for burials, or a burial ground attached: a register book of burials. It is not legally necessary, but in practice it is essential, to keep a careful map of the burial ground and to indicate in the register which space has been used for which burial. Failure to do so can lead to untold complications. The register is a register of earth burials within the churchyard or burial ground, not a register of occasions on which the burial service has been read over a body which is subsequently buried in a municipal cemetary, or which is subsequently cremated; nor is it a record of disposal of cremated remains. These services should not be entered in the burial register. They may, if desired, be recorded in the normal service register or (better) in a separate book kept for that purpose, but there is no legal need to do so, as they are not services of 'public worship' in the terms of the Canon or Measure. Cremations will be recorded in the crematorium register.

Copyright

If a parish wishes to have its own service booklets or leaflets printed, the copyright position must first be cleared.

BCP is Crown copyright, administered by Eyre and Spottiswoode (Publishers) Ltd., North Way, Andover, Hants SP10 5BE. Permission must be sought even for a service paper for use on a single occasion.

Copyright in ASB and other authorised alternative services is held on behalf of General Synod by the Central Board of Finance. For service papers used on a single occasion only, no permission is needed and no fee will be charged, provided that:

1. copies are not sold;
2. the name of the parish (etc.) with the date and description of the service is printed on the cover; and that
3. acknowledgement is printed in the following terms: '*The Alternative Service Book 1980*, material from which is included in this service, is copyright © The Central Board of Finance of the Church of England'.

If parishes or other users wish to reproduce material for use on more than one occasion, they must write for permission to The Legal Adviser to the General Synod, Church House, Great Smith Street, London SW1P 3NZ. Permission will usually only be given if the total service falls within legally permitted limits, and a fee (in 1988, £11.50 including VAT) will usually be charged for each permission.

If the service booklet is to include hymns by living authors, or authors who have been dead for less than fifty years, or extracts from translations of the Bible or Psalter, it is necessary to write to the publisher of the relevant hymn book, Bible, or Psalter to obtain copyright clearance. The Authorised Version of the Bible is Crown Copyright; enquire of Eyre and Spottiswoode at the address on page 25 above.

4

Morning and Evening Prayer

The minister

It is the duty of the incumbent either to be the minister of Morning or Evening Prayer or to invite some other person to do so. The invitation will normally be extended to a person holding the bishop's licence or permission to officiate, but in emergencies the minister or churchwardens may arrange for some other suitable lay person to do so (Canon B 11). Under this provision, a churchwarden could himself take the service if, for example, the incumbent suddenly fell ill and no-one else could be found. If the incumbent is incapacitated, or there is a vacancy in the benefice, the invitation should come from the churchwardens, though in practice arrangements are often made in these circumstances by the Rural Dean or diocesan Warden of Readers.

Under Canon B 43 (the 'ecumenical relations' canon), promulged in 1988, a minister or lay person who is a member in good standing of a Church designated for that purpose by the Archbishops of Canterbury and York (in practice, any of the 'main-stream' Churches except the Quakers and Salvationists, who do not administer the sacrament of baptism), and who is authorised to perform a

similar duty in his own Church, may be invited by the
incumbent to say or sing Morning or Evening Prayer, to
read the lessons, preach, or lead prayers. For the saying of
the Office and for preaching, the approval of the PCC has
to be obtained, and, if it is to be undertaken on a regular
basis, so must the approval of the bishop. (In Local
Ecumenical Projects, the provisions of Canon B 44 have
to be observed.) During a vacancy in the benefice, this
invitation must come from the Rural Dean, but the provisions as to the approval of the PCC and bishop still hold.

Vesture

The vesture of the minister of Morning or Evening
Prayer is laid down in Canon B 8. He should wear a
cassock, surplice, and scarf. If a graduate, he may add the
hood of his degree. On any appropriate occasion ('festal
best') he may wear a cope, in which case the scarf and
hood will be left off. Copes have no particular doctrinal
significance and serve simply to brighten the occasion.
Bands are optional and are not mentioned in the Canons.

Authorised forms

Currently authorised forms are 1662 (Book of Common
Prayer), 1872 (shortened forms of BCP allowed on weekdays by the Act of Uniformity (Amendment) Act of that
date), and 1980 (ASB). The 1872 forms are rarely (if ever)
met with, as they conform to no recognisable liturgical
principles.

In churches which use 1662, the seasonal openings sentences, invitation to worship, and absolution from the
1928 book are often still used. They had been incorporated within the 'Series 1' offices in the 1960s and so, by the
Bishops' ruling of 26 January 1988 (see p. 23 above) may
continue to be used where there is a well-established local
custom of doing so.

The pattern of the service

The Office is essentially a Ministry of the Word, so its centre is to be found in the Bible readings. We shall first deal with 1662 and then note the ASB variations.

Each service contains readings from both Testaments. They are separated, and flanked, by psalms and canticles, all of which (with the exception of *Te Deum*) are taken from Scripture. The Old Testament psalm comes before the Old Testament lesson, the canticle between the lessons is a 'bridge' linking the two Testaments, and the final canticle is an act of thanksgiving for the whole revelation of the complete Bible, the peak of which comes in our knowledge of Jesus the Christ. At Mattins this whole section is preceded by *Venite*, an invitation to worship God as the day begins.

The Ministry of the Word is the heart of the service. It is preceded by a section of preparation and followed by one of response. The preparation involves an opening sentence, invitation, confession, and absolution; the response is in terms of belief (the Creed) and of prayer (the intercessions). The first *Our Father* has been omitted in all revisions after 1872. Its 1662 position gives it no more exalted a function than that of a lick of glue to bind together the preparation and the Ministry of the Word. This is not good enough. Our Lord's own words are more significantly positioned as the high spot of the intercessions, led up to by the lesser litany and followed by the versicles and responses.

The sermon is not a necessary part of the BCP pattern, and the service proper ends with the Grace. On Sundays it is usually followed by hymns, a sermon, and the blessing.

The ASB. The ASB pattern is broadly similar to that of 1662, except that there is much more scope for the use of alternatives, some of which affect the order of sections within the service. For instance, note 3 on page 46 allows the penitential section to be used after the collects instead of at the beginning of the service, though it is to be doubted whether use is ever made of this particular option. Again, the sermon may either be associated with the readings by being placed immediately after the second lesson, or else it may be delivered at the end of the service, in which case it can be linked with the intercessions.

The language (as everywhere in the ASB) is simpler and the prayers shorter than in 1662. There is a wider choice of opening sentences and a new lectionary. The psalms may be said either according to the BCP monthly cycle (see p. 982, note 7) or according to the ASB's own cycle which gives a much smaller portion of psalmody to each service.

Both Morning and Evening Prayer in the ASB may be used in a longer or shorter form, though it is recommended (page 46, note 1) that the longer form be used on Sundays. Since, however, many sections of the longer form may be optionally omitted (and are marked by having blue rather than black paragraph numbers), there is little difference between the longer form with the maximum omissions and the shorter form as printed. (At Morning Prayer, the only difference is that there is in the shorter form no canticle between the two Scripture readings; at Evening Prayer, the shortened form omits one of the Scripture readings, the Creed, and the Collect of the Day.) In the shorter form, and optionally in the full form (see the table on page 72), particular canticles are assigned to each of the six weekdays. If the shorter forms are used, there are then three Scripture readings shared between the two services—one from the Old and two from the New Testament. In this case, the permission given in note 3 on page 981 allows the three readings allocated to the Holy Communion on that day to be used at the two daily offices instead.

The ASB also gives a litany and occasional prayers, and (on page 71) shows how Morning or Evening Prayer or the shortened form of Morning Prayer might be incorporated within a celebration of the Rite A Holy Communion.

The ASB offices of Morning and Evening Prayer, together with the collects, psalter, lectionary, and RSV Bible, are printed in a single composite volume as *A Daily Office Book* (Collins, 1986).

We will now go through the services and comment on some of the choices before the person who is taking them.

The Preparation

1662's opening sentences are purely penitential. The scope in ASB is much wider. There is a selection of general sentences on p. 47, and a seasonal choice on pp. 37–42. In addition, the note on p. 37 allows the introductory sentences provided with the Communion propers on pp. 398ff. to be used to preface the Office.

The 1662 introduction is often abbreviated, or replaced by that of 1928. This is less penitential and sets out well the reasons for coming together for worship. If it is used, remember that it ends with a call to kneel in silence. That silence ought to be long enought to be felt, and after it, it is as well to indicate to the congregation that it is over, by using the words 'Let us humbly confess . . .'. (1928 gives these words as an alternative to the invitation, but they are better made as an addition.)

There needs to be an agreed policy for the beginning of congregational prayers like the confession. In some churches, the 1662 policy ('saying after me') is adopted—the clergyman begins with the opening phrase and expects the congregation to repeat it after him and then continue the prayer under their own momentum. In other places, the minister begins the prayer and hopes that the congregation will catch up with him somehow and at some unspecified point. It is best for the leader to say the opening phrase and follow it with a pause of a fraction of a second as an indication to the congregation that they are to continue in unison. Provided that the congregation know what is expected of them (and they will soon pick it up) this is the neatest solution.

The absolution may only be spoken by a priest. If a layperson is taking the service, the absolution in BCP is replaced by the collect of Trinity 21, and in ASB the italicised words 'you' and 'your' are replaced by 'us', and 'our' (see note 4 on p. 46).

Canticles

Venite is the opening canticle at BCP Morning Prayer and is one of the ASB alternatives. If the 1662 Table of Psalms is used, *Venite* is omitted on the nineteenth morning on BCP and replaced by one of its alternatives in ASB. The Easter Anthems (printed in BCP immediately before the Collect of Easter Day and in ASB on pp. 51, 63, 74, and 86) are specified by BCP for Easter morning only and as an alternative at any time (morning or evening) by ASB. They are particularly appropriate in the Great Forty Days between Easter and Ascension, and—since every Sunday is a festival of the Resurrection—ASB (p. 72) suggests their use on Saturday evenings, to remind us of this as we prepare for Sunday.

The other alternative to *Venite* in the ASB is *Jubilate* (Ps. 100); evening invitatories are Ps. 134, *O Gladsome Light*, or the Easter Anthems.

The only guidance BCP gives about alternative canticles is that *Venite* and *Cantate Domino* cannot be used on the nineteenth day, nor *Deus misereatur* on the twelfth. It is customary in many places to use *Benedicite* instead of *Te Deum* in Lent, Advent, and on Wednesdays and Fridays. The ASB suggestions (which do not accord with this practice) are on p. 72. Rubric 15 on p. 55 suggests *Saviour of the World* for Lent; p. 72 more sensibly offers it as a weekly choice on Fridays and (less appropriately) Tuesdays. Some people feel that *Gloria in Excelsis* has for so many centuries been a Eucharistic hymn that the ASB is wrong in suggesting its use at Morning Prayer.

Note that the final verse of some ASB canticles (*A Song of Creation*, *Great and Wonderful*, *Bless the Lord*, and *Glory and Honour*) is un-numbered. This indicates that it should be treated in the same way as the *Gloria*.

Psalms

1662 gives a monthly cycle for the recitation of the psalms (given also on p. 1047 of ASB). ASB splits the psalter into smaller portions, and takes longer to cover the whole book. When the monthly cycle is used (see ASB, p. 1047), on the 31st day of the month, either the psalms for the 30th day are repeated, or we use the psalms of the monthly course which have been omitted on one of the previous Sundays. The ASB psalm cycle is given in the SPCK/Mowbray lectionary for each day.

The Prayer Book (Versions of the Bible) Measure 1965 applies to the psalter as it also applies to the readings at the Eucharist (but not to the lessons at the Office). Under it, any version of the Bible duly authorised by General Synod and approved by the PCC may be used. On any particular occasion, it is for the minister to make his choice from the permitted alternatives. General Synod has authorised these versions of the psalter: AV, RV, RSV, NEB, Jerusalem Bible, Good News Bible (Today's English Version), BCP psalter (Coverdale), Revised Psalter, and the Liturgical Psalter as printed in ASB. The NIV psalter and Grail Psalter are not authorised for use in BCP services in substitution for psalms there printed out in full.

Lessons

Versions. Any Bible version may be used at Morning or Evening Prayer at the discretion of the minister providing that the bishop is satisfied that it is doctrinally sound. Before deciding on any particular version, read it out aloud in church. Some versions are better for private study than public reading, and some buildings are more suited to grandeur and less colloquial language than others. If the members of the congregation read the lessons in their own Bibles (a habit much to be encouraged), then use that version wherever possible for public reading and only make a substitution on rare occasions and for good reasons.

Announcing the lessons. The 1662 use ('Here beginneth such a verse of such a chapter of such a book') is unhelpful in the extreme. The ASB order (book, chapter, verse—see note 7 on p. 46) is much to be preferred. Use the titles of the books as given in the version you are reading, or at least adopt a consistent scheme. Remember that it is 'The book of the prophet Isaiah' or 'The book of the prophecy of Isaiah'; 'The book of the Acts of the Apostles'; 'The book of the revelation to John'; and 'The book Genesis', not 'The book of Genesis'.

Keep silence at the end of the lesson, long enough for the congregation to reflect on it. If there is only a pause of a few seconds, let it be between the last words of the reading and 'here ends the first reading' rather than between the announcement and the next canticle.

Reading the lessons. The choice of reader is vital. If the lesson is the high point of the Office, it *must* be audible and intelligible. The voice must be clear, precise, and used at the right pitch and speed; and this cannot often be found without prior rehearsal in the church building itself. It is a common fault to read far too rapidly. Speed depends partly upon the resonance of the building (and that in turn often depends on whether the building is full or empty), partly on the voice of the reader (a bass voice needs to go more slowly than a treble), and partly on the passage being read. Narrative can take a faster pace than close argumentation or profound truths. For instance, in the Prologue to St John's Gospel, the words 'there was a man sent from God, whose name was John' can be read much faster than the words 'the Word was made flesh, and dwelt among us'; and the variation in pace will make for a more interesting reading. On the whole, the Synoptic Gospels can be read much faster than the Epistles. Dramatic pauses only become effective if used sparingly. The tendency to drop the voice to inaudibility at the end of a phrase or sentence needs watching. Some words are important and need emphasising; but we have all heard parodies of the man who is so intent on emphasising every word that the whole performance becomes ludicrous. On the other hand, every word should be clear—even unaccented phrases like 'it is', or words like 'the' and 'and' must not be muttered or elided. And the pauses for punctuation and breath *must* come in the right place if the sense is not to be destroyed. I still remember from adolescence a clergyman who always read the Comfortable Words in the form 'God-so-loved-the-world-that-he-gave-his-only-begotten-Son-to-the-end,   (pause   for breath) that-all-that-believe-in-him . . .', etc.

Lectionaries. Most people will be content to let the compilers of the SPCK/Mowbrays printed lectionary for the year work out all the complications, and will take the readings as there set out. There are two lectionaries commonly in use; BCP and ASB. The large edition of the lectionary prints both, on facing pages. It is wiser to stick to one or the other for a year at a time; to dodge between the two can lead to unnecessary repetitions—for example, the BCP Gospel for Epiphany 2 is the same as the ASB Year 1 Gospel for Epiphany 3.

A brief sentence before the reading helps those less familiar with the Bible than they should be, to 'latch on' to the context and thrust of the passage. This should not be a full-scale commentary nor a substitute for the sermon, and ought to be worked out (and written down) before the service begins.

The Creed

Note that the wording of the Apostles' Creed in ASB differs from the 1662 translation.

1662 demands that on thirteen specified occasions each

year the *Quicunque vult* (alias the 'Athanasian Creed')
should replace the Apostles' Creed at Morning Prayer.
This is not a rubric generally observed. The confident
certainties of the *Quicunque* on highly metaphysical questions are not nowadays popular, and its damnatory clauses
ensured that in the ASB it sank without trace.

Collects

ASB has a much richer provision than BCP. The Collects
are given (together with the sentences and the Eucharistic
readings) in four blocks:

(a) Sundays and Seasons (pp. 397–750) covering the
    same days as BCP (though on a different basis) with
    the addition of the Second Sunday after Christmas.

(b) Festivals and Holy Days (pp. 751–826), or the 'Red-
    Letter' days. Notice that they are not all on the BCP
    days—St Matthias has moved from 24 February to 14
    May and St Thomas from 21 December to 3 July. ASB
    adds St Joseph (19 March), SS Peter and Paul for 29
    June if desired in place of St Peter alone, St Mary
    Magdalen (22 July), the Transfiguration (6 August),
    the Blessed Virgin Mary (8 September), and provi-
    sions for the dedication, consecration, or patronal
    feast or feast of title.

(c) Lesser Festivals and Holy Days (pp. 827–901); a
    miscellaneous collection. Some of the lesser saints in
    the Calendar have ASB propers; most have not. In
    their case, use the 'common' forms from pp. 844–878,
    which are for martyrs, teachers (called 'doctors' in the
    BCP Calendar), bishops, abbots or abbesses, mis-
    sionaries, or 'of any saint'. If a saint is described in the
    Calendar under more than one of these categories, it
    is customary to use the common for the last category
    named. Thus Ambrose (7 December) is described as a
    Bishop and Teacher, so his collect is the common of a
    teacher rather than of a bishop. Those who want to

use propers rather than commons for all or any of these lesser saints will find ample material in *The Cloud of Witnesses* (Collins, for the Alcuin Club, 1982), compiled by Martin Draper with collects by G. B. Timms. Each saint has a brief biographical paragraph, sentences, collect, psalm, and readings (including a reading by or about the saint in question).

(d) Various Occasions (pp. 903–978). These are worth listing, and may provide material for special as well as annual occasions. By custom, the unity of the Church (p. 904) is prayed for during the week of 18–25 January, the missionary work of the Church (p. 906) is remembered on 29 November (St Andrew's Eve), and thanksgiving is made for the institution of Holy Communion (p. 920) on the Thursday after Trinity Sunday; but there are plenty of other occasions on which these collects will be appropriate.

The ASB Collects, of course, are in modern language; they are now available gathered together in a separate booklet, *ASB Collects*, published jointly by SPCK and Mowbray. Those who wish to use them, but in 'thou' form, will find them in *The Collects: Traditional Language* (Church House Publishing, 1987). This is, however, primarily designed for use, not with ASB Morning or Evening Prayer, but with the Rite B Eucharist.

When more than one holy day falls on the same date or when a holy day falls on a Sunday, precedence is determined by the Rules to Order the Service. For BCP, these are the 1973 rules given in all printings of BCP since that date; the ASB rules are on pp. 26–29. They are complicated and most people let the year's SPCK/Mowbrays Lectionary do their calculations for them. In it, praetermitted saints' days (i.e. those which have been omitted for that year because they fall on greater festivals) are given in square brackets. The praetermission may need to be disregarded for local reasons, when a local or patron saint would otherwise go uncommemorated that year.

Despite the rules, there is a case for transferring a red-letter day to a neighbouring Sunday. The congregation will be bigger on the Sunday, and the opportunity of teaching about that particular saint will not then be lost. The same goes for weekday celebrations. If a church normally only has one mid-week celebration and there is a red-letter day during that week, why not transfer it to the day when there is already going to be a Eucharist and there is therefore likely to be a ready-made congregation?

The BCP rule is to use the Sunday collect on the preceding Saturday evening and the collect of a red-letter day on its eve, but it is nowadays not customary to observe eves in this way. Similarly, there used to be a multiplicity of collects on saints' days, with rules about whether to use the Sunday collect or not, and if so, which collect came first. Such liturgical niceties may now be left to those who take an interest in them; the aim is to have one collect, and one alone, as the Collect of the Day (see ASB, p. 32, note 7). The BCP practice of having the seasonal collect after the Collect of the Day during Advent and Lent and in Christmas week is not followed by ASB.

Note, incidentally, that 'for' is used to indicate the subject of a collect, and 'of' to indicate its occasion. Thus we speak of 'the Collect *for* Purity' at Holy Communion, but 'the Collect *of* Christmas Day'.

Intercessions

In this part of the service, the minister has his head. Let him, for that very reason, take great pains in preparation. Over three hundred years ago, Bishop Cosin bade his readers 'avoid, as near as might be, all extemporal effusions of irksome and indigested prayers'. He, being dead, yet speaketh. Extempore prayers need to be very carefully controlled if they are not to get out of hand and become wearisomely repetitive. If the minister favours them, let him at least write down the headings of his intercessions beforehand, and look at the pattern of them over a few weeks to see whether he is not caught on a small treadmill of favourite concerns. And, *please*, avoid such wheedling language to the Almighty as the phrase 'We do just ask you, Lord, . . .'.

Better than extempore prayers is the use of biddings. Remember that a bidding is addressed to the congregation, not to God, whereas a prayer is offered to God and not spoken to the congregation. Incongruities (frequently heard in the ASB Eucharistic intercessions) can be avoided if the minister has clearly in his mind whom he is speaking to, and keeps to that form of address until the bidding is over and the prayer begins. Biddings are useful because, being addressed to the congregation, they can be used without having to give God information he presumably already has. 'Let us pray for Tuesday's PCC meeting' is better than 'Lord, thou knowest that there is a meeting of the PCC on Tuesday next at the Vicarage'.

It helps if the intercessions follow a regular pattern. The pattern of the State Prayers is the Queen (governments, the affairs of the world), the Church (the religious needs of mankind), ourselves. That of the General Intercession, as broken into sections on p. 103 of the ASB, is a useful one. The Rite A Eucharistic intercessions can just as well be used at Morning or Evening Prayer as at Holy Communion.

When set prayers are being used, bear a number of points in mind. The first is that the congregation have a great deal to do in a set prayer. They have to hear what is being said, to think out what the phrase means, and to turn it into prayer. If an unfamiliar prayer is said at top speed there will be no time to do all this and the congregation will give up. But it is equally unsatisfactory simply to slow up the delivery of the prayer in a uniform manner. The prayer will contain phrases and concepts which are

unities. Each of these should be spoken clearly and without rush (but equally without drag), and the pause for
reflection should follow, before the next phrase is started.
The pause need not be more than a second; but it is
essential. It is easier to get into the habit of doing this
when prayers are printed out in lines rather than as
continuous prose.

It is perhaps even more important to take time over a
prayer when it is familiar than when it is new to a
congregation. Familiarity and contempt are frequent bed-
fellows, and the careful and measured use of a well-known
prayer, with pauses for reflection, helps to guard against
this danger. Particularly is this true of prayers like the
Grace, which is so readily recognised simply as a formula
for saying 'the intercessions are going to end as soon as
this prayer is finished' that it is difficult to get any real
praying done through it.

On the other hand, the frequent use of particular
prayers is not to be despised. They become loved and can
be filled with personal content by their very repetition.
The biddings or introductions can be the variable part of
the intercessions, and the prayers themselves can be familiar formulae. BCP contains a considerable treasury of
prayers; its collects can be used as foci for intercession
through the year, not only on the Sunday for which they
are set. Time spent going through the Prayer Book and
classifying the collects according to subject matter is not
wasted, and ASB already contains (on pp. 109–112) a
subject index of its prayers. Incidentally, if you are using a
familar prayer in public, it is unnecessarily irritating to
alter or expand its wording.

Each minister will have his own favourite anthology of
prayers for use in church. Try to use prayers whose
sobriety of tone makes them suitable for public use. Many
excellent prayers are more suited to private devotion than
to speaking out loud. Emotional phrases ('gallant and
high-hearted happiness') put the minister on a knife-edge;

it is so easy to slip into embarrassing bathos. Useful collections are *Parish Prayers* ('thou'-language) and *Contemporary Parish Prayers* ('you'-language, and set out line by line), compiled by Frank Colquhoun (Hodder and Stoughton, originally 1967 and 1975 but frequently reprinted). F. B. MacNutt's *Prayer Manual*, though first published in 1951, has proved its lasting power, and its fourth edition was brought out in 1986 (Mowbrays, paperback). David Silk's *Prayers for use at the Alternative Services* (Mowbrays, revised edition 1986) is widely used.

If it is done properly, prayer is hard work. This goes for the congregation as well as for the leader. For this reason, the prayers at the Office should be carefully chosen and few in number. 1662 gives five, including the Grace, and this is a good number to take for a norm.

The Litany

BCP prescribes the litany after Morning Prayer on Wednesdays, Fridays, and Sundays, and as 'commanded by the Ordinary'. The ASB litany (pp. 99–102) gives no such instructions, but if it is used at Morning Prayer, it replaces the whole of the Office from the end of the Creed onwards. As long as sections I and VI are used, the rest may be treated selectively.

Those who use the BCP litany may like to consider some minor amendments. To add a comma, as 1928 does, in the opening phrase ('O God, the Father, of heaven') indicates that what is being signified is name and address rather than paternity and filiation. The petition about 'sudden death' may be altered, as in ASB, to 'dying unprepared'. No one wants to linger, but all Christians should pray that death may not find them unready to meet their Maker. 'The Lords of the Council, and all the nobility' became, in 1928, 'The High Court of Parliament, and all the ministers of the Crown'. 'Fruits' of the spirit should go into the singular, to agree with Gal 5.22. The mention of travellers 'by land, or by water' is too limiting for today's possibilities. Either leave out those five words, or follow the example of the 1976 Prayer Book of the American Episcopal Church which speaks of 'all who are in danger by reason of their labor or their travel'.

Many other forms of litany are to be found in books or pamphlets. They need to be used with care. If the congregation have copies, well and good. If not, they have to make the effort of remembering what the response is to what versicle, and in consequence they frequently give up. The following rules are useful:

1. Tell the people beforehand what the response is, and what the versicle. Wherever possible, let it be a familiar one so that it is automatic and does not need consciously to be borne in mind throughout the litany.

2. Do not change the response in the course of the litany unless absolutely necessary, and certainly not after only two or three times' use.

3. Make the suffrages short so that the versicle and response come frequently and establish a rhythm.

4. If there is to be a pause for making the suffrages one's own, let it be between suffrage and versicle, not between the response and the next suffrage.

Sermon

The congregation at Mattins or Evensong is often very different in character from that at the Parish Eucharist. There are generally few children present, and the structure is such as to make it possible to devote a greater time to the sermon than can be done at Parish Communion. The Office can therefore be used for more sustained and serious instruction in the Christian faith for those who are committed to it but who need help in their understanding of it if they are effectively to grasp it or to commend it to the folk around them.

Whether the sermon as such is the best vehicle for doing

this, is a question too large for the scope of this book. There are alternative ways of using the 'spot' in the liturgy meant for declaring the message of Scripture and applying it to the life of the congregation. The present author has discussed some of them on pp. 55–6 of *The Paradox of Worship* (SPCK, 1977). But the question needs to be asked whether, if the Sunday evening session aims to instruct and empower Christians to be Christ's ambassadors during the week ahead, Evensong with sermon is the best way to do it. There are many other possibilities. A brief period of worship could be followed by a talk with questions, refreshments, and discussion. There could be a debate on some subject of current concern, or a parish meeting or conference on policy. The congregation could shut down for a few weeks and convene instead as a series of house groups. There could be an evangelistic 'guest service' at which each member of the congregation is asked to bring along a non-churchgoer. There could be a totally informal session of Prayer and Praise at which the worshippers shared their deepest concerns together before the Lord. There could be healing services. The scope for experiment is endless, and all possibilities need to be considered by an incumbent who complains that Evensong has 'gone dead' on him and his dwindling afternoon or evening congregation. The purpose of the programme at this time of a Sunday, however, must be borne in mind. What is being designed is not entertainment but training for Christian living within a worshipping context. That *ought* to be fun, and if the zest has gone out of it, reconsideration is necessary.

Blessing

Morning or Evening Prayer usually ends with the blessing. This can be the Aaronic blessing from Numbers 6.24–6, or the dismissal from the Series 1 (1928) Confirmation service ('Go forth into the world in peace; . . .'), or the appropriate seasonal blessing from Rite A in the ASB (pp. 159–161), or one of the two forms given as prayers 18 and 19 on p. 107 of the ASB, or a blessing from the priest's favourite book of prayers. Deacons or Readers modify the declaratory wording from the 'God bless you' form to the 'May God bless us' form.

Compline

There are many occasions (particularly with small groups) when it is appropriate to offer brief prayers at the end of a day. Compline has proved its value on such occasions. There is an order in the 1928 book, but more people use one or other of the forms published by Mowbrays: *The Office of Compline after the Ancient Order* is in 'thou'-form, whilst *The Office of Compline, an Alternative Order* is in more modern language, and is available either plain (by David Silk) or as a music edition (by David Silk and Brother Reginald SSF). There is also an ASB-type form freely based on Compline under the heading *Night Prayer* (published jointly by CHP and Mowbray) in a separate booklet as well as on pp. 58–69 of *Lent, Holy Week, Easter* (commended by the House of Bishops and published by Church House Publishing, Cambridge University Press, and SPCK, 1986).

5

Holy Communion: Preliminaries

The minister

According to Canons B 12 and C 1, only priests of the Church of England or Churches 'whose orders are recognised and accepted by the Church of England' may 'consecrate and administer' the Holy Communion. The other Churches referred to are those of the Anglican Communion and certain others with which the Church of England is in full communion. In cases of doubt, ask your diocesan office, or the Archbishop of Canterbury's Department of Ecumenical Affairs at Lambeth Palace, London SE1 7JU. Within a Local Ecumenical Project, the bishop's rulings made under Canon B 44 must be observed.

The word 'administer' in Canon B 12 does not refer to what is sometimes loosely called the 'administration' of the bread and cup to the communicants, but to what is generally known as 'celebrating' the Eucharist. The distribution of the sacrament to the people is reserved to the priests and deacons and such people 'specially authorised to do so by the bishop acting under such regulations as the General Synod may make from time to time'. Bishops may authorise deaconesses and lay workers to do so at the invitation of the incumbent concerned (Canons D 1 and

E 7)—not by virtue of their office but by virtue of the bishop's licence in that respect. The bishop may also issue permissions (either direct or through an archdeacon) to other lay persons (Canon B 12). These licences and permissions allow the person concerned to act under the direction of and at the invitation of the incumbent who has absolute discretion when and whether to do so. They cover the distribution both of bread and cup.

The minister may invite a lay person to read the epistle or gospel. No episcopal permission is needed unless the diocese has its own regulations on the matter.

Canon B 43 allows ministers and lay people of other denominations who are baptised and in good standing in their own communion to preach, read the scriptures, take the intercessions, or assist at the distribution. Their Churches must profess the doctrine of the Trinity and administer the sacraments of baptism and Holy Communion, and the individual concerned must be capable of performing a similar function in his own Church. The minister invites, but first, in the case of assisting at the distribution at any time or of preaching on a regular basis, he must obtain the approval of the bishop, and the PCC's approval must also be given if anyone is to be invited to preach or distribute the elements under the provisions of Canon B 43. In a Local Ecumenical Project, B 44 must be observed.

Communicants

Communion may be given to members of the Church of England who have been confirmed, or are 'ready and desirous to be confirmed'. The phrase 'ready and desirous' has not been legally defined, but it would (for example) certainly include the person who was prepared for confirmation, missed the service through illness, and was waiting for the next opportunity of being confirmed.

Canon B 15 A allows communion to be given to baptised and communicant members of other Trinitarian

Churches if they are in good standing in their own Church. If a person receives communion under these provisions over a long period of time which appears likely to continue indefinitely, the incumbent is bidden to set before him the normal requirements of the Church of England with regard to communicant status. In cases of doubt, the bishop's ruling is final.

Any baptised person in danger of death may receive the Holy Communion, and no questions asked.

If the clergyman believes that a person who presents himself to receive the Holy Communion is in 'malicious and open contention with his neighbours' or guilty of 'other grave and open sin without repentance', and wishes for that reason to deny him the sacrament, he should weigh the matter carefully. The procedure to be followed is laid down in Canon B 16, but it must be emphasised that a clergyman can very easily get himself into very deep water indeed. The aggrieved person could start a lawsuit claiming defamation of character. He does not need to prove that he was actually repelled from the Lord's Table; in certain circumstances it is sufficient for him to show that the clergyman intimated that if he were to present himself at the altar rail, he would be refused the sacrament. Priests tempted to take this line of action are strongly advised to consult a solicitor or the diocesan legal adviser (and must, except 'in case of grave and immediate scandal', inform the bishop) before taking any action.

Vesture

Officially, the Church of England attaches no particular doctrinal significance to any particular vesture allowed by Canon. Despite this, the minister must not change the form of vesture used in a church where he officiates unless he has ascertained by consultation with the PCC that such change will be acceptable. If there is disagreement, the bishop's directions have to be obeyed (Canon B 8).

The Eucharistic agenda

When a Christian community comes together for Eucharistic worship, there are five items on the agenda:

1. to adore God and sing his praises;
2. to listen to his Word;
3. to pray for each other and for the world;
4. to cleanse the consciences of the worshippers;
5. to do with bread and wine what Jesus commanded.

The final item can in its turn be divided into a fourfold action—taking, blessing, breaking, and sharing.

All these elements will be present in the Eucharist, though they will not always be clearly marked off from each other. In 1662, for example, the bread and wine are put on the table as though we were about to begin the Ministry of the Sacrament, but they are left there without further comment whilst the intercessions, confession, and absolution take place. There are many people who wish to see the Eucharistic rite structured so as to separate the various items on the agenda; the congregation can then see at any moment where they have got to in the rite and how each part of the service is related to the whole pattern of the Eucharistic agenda. People like this will be happier with ASB than with BCP, though if they wish to have a service closer to BCP in its pattern whilst using contemporary forms of speech, they will find it by using the ASB Rite A up to page 125 and then continuing on pp. 146–53.

The Rites

1662 is virtually invariant except for propers and the choice of prayer for the Queen, post-communion prayer, and offertory sentences. The newer rites provide an almost bewildering selection of opportunities for variation.

The two 'families' of rites in ASB are Rite A and Rite B. During the 1960s and 1970s, three sets of alternative services were authorised for experimental use. Series

1 derived from the proposals set forth in Church Assembly in 1928, but which never received parliamentary authorisation; Series 2 was a new production, in 'thou' language, and Series 3 was in 'you' form. Rite A is the successor to Series 3, and Rite B comes from a revision and collation of Series 1 and 2. Thus the Rite B first intercession, thanksgiving, and post-communion prayer (sections 17, 30, and 46) are from Series 1, and the second alternatives (sections 18, 31, and 47) derive from Series 2.

Rites A and B share a number of departures from BCP. The *Gloria in Excelsis* may come at the beginning of the service instead of preceding the blessing. There is provision for an Old Testament lesson in addition to the Epistle. There is an entirely new set of collects and lections specially prepared for use with the ASB rites (though the BCP ones may be used with Rite B—see note 4 on p. 177). The sermon immediately follows the Gospel so that the word read and the word preached may be the more closely associated, and the Creed then follows the sermon as the encapsulated doctrine of both lections and sermon. There are new prayers of intercession, which may be broken into paragraphs by a versicle and response, and the scope of the intercessions (for Church and world) is wider than the BCP's 'Christ's Church militant here in earth'. For those called upon to lead the intercessions at Holy Communion, where ASB Rite A or B is used, several useful booklets are available, published by Mowbray, including: *Intercessions at the Eucharist* by Raymond Chapman, and *Intercessions at the Parish Communion* by William C. Collins. The Prayer of Humble Access does not intrude within the crescendo beginning with the Preface and continuing into the Prayer of Consecration. The ablutions may be taken immediately after the communion of the people, instead of (as in BCP) having to wait until after the blessing.

The first alternatives in Rite B also permit an arrangement formerly known as the 'Interim Rite' whereby, without departing more than necessary from the prayers and order of BCP, something both of the form and significance of the ancient Canon of the Mass may be restored. Before the ASB, this used to be effected by following the BCP Prayer of Consecration immediately by the Prayer of Oblation (beginning it 'Wherefore, O Lord and heavenly Father, we thy humble servants . . .') and the Lord's Prayer. Then came the communion of the people and the BCP Prayer of Thanksgiving (i.e. 'Almighty and everliving God, we most heartily thank thee . . .'). In Rite B, this is achieved by removing the words 'here we present unto thee . . . ourselves . . .' from the Prayer of Oblation, but using the rest of that prayer as a continuation of the Prayer of Consecration. Then the self-oblation is allowed in paragraph 46 as part of a post-communion prayer. This means that although we offer 'this our sacrifice of praise and thanksgiving' within the Prayer of Consecration, the oblation of ourselves as a living sacrifice is not made until the communicants have been joined with Christ in his sacramental presence.

There are other points on which the new rites lay stress which are not in 1662. They make mention of the resurrection and ascension within the Eucharistic prayer, so that the rite as a whole is less exclusively Calvary-centred. The work of the Holy Spirit is emphasised in such phrases as 'grant that by the power of your Holy Spirit these gifts of bread and wine may be to us his body and his blood', and 'renew us by your Spirit'. The note of joy is emphasised in the Acclamations and the congregational cry of 'blessing and honour and glory and power'.

The new rites also move away from a theology of a 'moment of consecration'. It is the whole Eucharistic action, not one prayer or one formula within one prayer, which effects the consecration of the elements. So the central prayer (although it is called the Prayer of Consecration in Rite B section 29) is known as the Thanksgiving in Rite B sections 30 and 31, and the Eucharistic

Prayer in Rite A. By its provisions for the consecration of additional bread or wine if supplies run out during the administration, BCP seems to say that the words of institution are a formula of consecration. Both Rites A and B guard against that by ensuring that the formula in such a case uses no words from the Eucharistic prayer. For a similar reason, the second thanksgiving of Rite B has reduced the manual acts within the Eucharistic prayer and Rite A omits them altogether (though note 16 on page 117 allows 'the traditional manual acts' if desired).

But the most important thing about the ASB rites is the way in which the items of the 'Eucharistic agenda' have been clearly separated and pointed up. The 'staging' of the rite ought to help to make this even more clear.

Geography and ceremonial

As we said in our Introduction, this book is not a ceremonial guide. The reader will have to look elsewhere for detailed directions about liturgical choreography. Nonetheless, there must be some general guidance, because ceremonial is inescapable in a service whose essence lies in what is *done*. The choice is not between ceremonial and no ceremonial, but between ceremonial which is appropriate to the mystery which it is intended to show forth and ceremonial which obscures it (see the present author's *The Paradox of Worship*, SPCK, 1977, pp. 99–102). There is ceremonial in standing at the north side of the Holy Table clad in surplice and black scarf, just as there is ceremonial in a High Mass with all the stops out. Both can be done sloppily and carelessly or with simple dignity.

If the Eucharistic agenda can be transformed into a Eucharistic drama, then the congregation will be helped to see what is going on and to participate in it more intelligently. 'Drama' makes us think of the stage, and it is not wrong to think of the 'stage management' of the

Eucharist. After all, unless the words of the dramatist are brought to life by the producer, the message of a play will not get across to the audience: and in the Eucharist we are taking part in something of much greater importance than a play. Let us therefore help the participants engage in it with understanding.

Remember that the celebrant is at a distance from the congregation. If they are to appreciate his words and his movements, he must bear this distance in mind. The advice we have already given to the lesson-reader at the Office (pp. 40–41 above) is doubly relevant to the Eucharistic celebrant. If he cannot get help from a friend skilled in elocution or amateur dramatics, let him at least seek a candid helper who can tell him where and why he is failing to communicate effectively through inaudibility or odd mannerisms. If possible, let him do this early in his ministry, for bad habits are the harder to erase the longer they have been indulged.

For a similar reason, gestures at the altar need to be slower and bigger than they should be in close-up. If you are going to elevate the host, then remember the mediaeval cry of 'Heave it higher, Sir priest!' An elevation of an inch or two serves as a private devotion to the priest but it is something of which the congregation are completely unaware. If you want the congregation to be at one with you in your devotion at this point, then lift the chalice and host above your head so that they may see that a significant action has been performed; and keep the position for some seconds before lowering your hands.

Always bear in mind the effect on the congregation of any action of the priest. If you are at the east side of the altar facing the congregation, there will not be a cross on the altar—not even a small one. Nor will you genuflect, as this will make you bob out of sight for an undignified moment. If you bow instead of genuflecting, your bow will be a deep and slow one, not a quick dip of the head as if you were a hen pecking for grain. If the table is in full view of the people, it must not be cluttered up with an excess of impedimenta. Some other place must be found for sermon notes, spectacle cases, hymn and prayer books, music copies, parish magazines, and the weekly notice-sheet. The table should have (Canon F 2) a fair white linen cloth on it, together with the necessary vessels, and the service book (on a cushion or stand if necessary). If there are no freestanding candlesticks at either side of the table, there may need to be a pair upon it. But that is all. Other places, not in the congregation's direct view, must be found for everything else.

The three-act drama

The Eucharistic drama has three acts. If they can centre on three different parts of the church, then the message of the structure of the rite will be spelt out more clearly to the congregation.

The Liturgy of the Word is concerned mainly with the readings and sermon. The table has nothing to do with this part of the service, and should therefore at this stage be left alone. The priest either takes his place in his stall in the choir, or has a seat to one side or other of the table if the sanctuary is big enough to allow this without a sense of clutter. There is no need to have two lecterns and a pulpit, although if there are, then the Old Testament lesson and Epistle are read from the south lectern and the Gospel from the north. It would be better for all to be read from a position in the centre, as close to the people as possible, to aid audibility. If there is to be a Gospel procession, then let it come right among the people, to the nave aisle. There is no adequate symbolism in moving a few steps north from the centre of the altar.

The prayers are the prayers of the whole Church and are therefore most appropriately led from the nave, as far back in the centre aisle as is convenient. Neither the lectern nor the pulpit are suitable. They have other functions and should be reserved for these.

There are three possible places for the celebrant to

stand for the Liturgy of the Sacrament:

1. To obey the 1662 rubric and to stand on the north side of the table enables the congregation to see what is going on. Unfortunately, it has in the past been degraded into something of a party shibboleth. Mercifully, such indications of churchmanship are becoming things of the past, and many Evangelicals prefer the eastward-facing position.

2. If the celebrant faces the people, he must know why he does it. If it is to symbolise that he and his congregation form a circle round the altar, then it is no good at all if the table is at the far end of a long chancel and the congregation is glued to the back pews. The westward-facing position has become so much of a fetish that it has often been adopted in churches where the whole geography of the sanctuary cries out in protest. The physical constraints of the church building always need to be borne in mind when planning the choreography of the liturgy. The DAC can often offer advice which will not always involve petitioning for a faculty, since sometimes the interior of the church neither can nor should be re-ordered.

3. There are churches in which the celebrant has to continue facing east; the high altar cannot be re-designed and there is no room for a nave altar without ruining the visual impact of the building. When this is the case, the best use must be made of meaningful positioning in the Ministry of the Word and the intercessions. The altar can be even more dramatically reserved for the Ministry of the Sacrament in such a case.

Servers

Servers are not merely decorative; they help. A properly-run group of servers can take a load of concern off the celebrant's mind and enable him to concentrate on his own liturgy within the service with the minimum of distraction.

The servers, under their Head Server, should be responsible for a duty roster covering every Eucharist. In some churches, the Head Server trains the new recruits, but there is much to be said for the view that it is a duty of such importance that it can only be done adequately by the priest who is to be served.

As with an iceberg, so with a server's work. There is more unseen than seen. Unless there is a sacristan, the server should be responsible for getting the vessels out, making them up, laying out the vestments, counting out the breads, preparing the credence, and lighting the candles. Afterwards the server should extinguish the candles, clear the altar and the credence, put away, and leave everything ready for the server at the next Eucharist.

In some churches, the server joins in with the priest in their preparatory devotion at the altar before the service begins. An order for this is to be found in the Appendix of the 1928 book; other forms, involving a mutual confession between priest and server, are available on card. The popularity of this is waning. What is said and done in church should be said and done by and for and with the whole congregation. If the priest and server are to prepare themselves devotionally for the conduct of the service (and there is much to be said in favour of this), then let them do so in private, either at a side altar or in the vestry.

There is another way in which there is more unseen than seen to the business of being a server. That is in connection with the server's devotional life. His (or her) hidden life should be encouraged and fed by the work done around the altar. No less than the celebrant, the server is in a position of spiritual danger. He can either get blasé with holy things, or else use a familiarity with the externals of the sanctuary to bring him closer to the real heart of the matter. The demeanour of the priest in the vestry is of prime importance by way of example. A flippant attitude, even an over-hearty attitude, may encourage our servers to believe that we are merely play-acting when we are in public view. We *are* acting, in that we need to be aware of the rules of drama, but in the deeper sense we can never be actors only, for we are performing something in dread earnest to the honour and glory of almighty God. We cannot be unchanged through the experience of participating in public worship, whether as priest, as server, or as the member of a congregation. We may either grow in grace or become Gospel-hardened. Watch and pray.

A useful book to give to a server is *The Server's Handbook* by Lester Yeo (Religious and Moral Education Press, 1984), based on ASB Rite A.

Altar linen

It is helpful to have a group of ladies forming an Altar Linen Guild or guild of broderers. This group can be in charge of the supply and laundry of linen so that the priest never has to worry about a supply of clean and decent purificators or whether the linen cloth is wearing threadbare. They may be financed directly from the PCC but they will probably prefer to make themselves financially independent through coffee mornings and the like. They can then purchase altar requisites and repair frontals, robes, burses and veils—and make kneelers and even branch out into such examples of the broderer's art as bookmarks, pulpit falls, vestments, and frontals. The supply of bread and wine is reserved under Canon B 17 to the churchwardens with the advice and direction of the minister, but there is no reason why they should not delegate this duty.

Choosing between alternatives

1662 is a service where the scope for the exercise of the celebrant's discretion is minimal, but each of the ASB services consists of a skeleton of 'shall' with a considerable amount of 'may'. Not every clergyman seems to appreciate this. It is all too common to come to a church and find the whole of Rite A being used with the inclusion of every option, and sometimes reading 'both/and' when the text says 'either/or', as if the service had not been performed properly unless everything that could conceivably be put into it had been found a place. This is an unintelligent use of the possibilities of variation. What is a more excellent way?

First look at the service and mark up its invariable skeleton—those parts which must be said, however brief the service. In the ASB rites they are marked by having their paragraph numbers in black. Even within this basic skeleton, there is choice possible—most notably in the alternative intercessions, or the two Eucharistic Prayers of Rite B, or the four of Rite A. Note, however, that although prefatory note 7 to Rite B (p. 177) states that the use of the first intercession does not presume the use of the first Thanksgiving, it would make an oddly hybrid rite if any other permutation or combination than either 17 with the first part of 20, followed by 30 and 46, or else 18 with the second part of 20, plus 31 and 47, were to be used.

Once this skeleton has been identified, nothing should be added to it without first asking why. A liturgy should not be allowed to build up thoughtlessly—each part of it has a purpose, and the people who include that part must include it because they considered its purpose and approve of it. Sometimes the purpose in including an option within the ASB has been to satisfy the Evangelicals or to satisfy the Catholics or to satisfy those who could not bear to lose a loved and familiar prayer, and this conservatism should not be denigrated. But it should be recognised and allowed for, not let slip in covertly. The use of familar formulae may sometimes be the only way to ease in a new service, by including sufficient of the old to maintain the loyalty of those who do not like too much change too quickly. Newspaper typographers know the value of this approach. Look at your daily paper today, then go to the library to consult a copy of it of forty years ago, and the difference in appearance will amaze you. But you will find that the changes, radical though they have been in their totality, have been introduced almost unnoticeably, here a little and there a little. The people of this world can teach parish liturgists a great deal of practical wisdom if we let them.

Sometimes options should be regarded as alternative to each other, though the text may not say so in so many words. The *Kyries* and the *Gloria* at the beginning of the rite are like this: to have both is odd, but not unknown. It would be well to follow the hint in note 8 on p. 116 of the ASB and reserve the *Gloria* as a festal alternative to the *Kyries* rather than to make it an everyday feature of the service (remembering that every Sunday is a festival of the Resurrection). The notes in the next chapter will show how services of different 'feel' can be built up by the use of a different selection of alternatives.

Agapé and Eucharist

We can tell from 1 Cor. 11 that originally the Holy Communion was celebrated as part of a meal. At an early stage this meal or agapé was separated from the Eucharist; when regulations forbade communal meals of societies, it was the agapé which was discontinued so that the Eucharist alone remained.

Nowadays, when the church meets for a meal—harvest supper, stewardship dinner, or the like—all Eucharistic overtones are absent. Could we not restore the Eucharistic significance of a common meal shared between Christians? The Ministry of the Word could precede the meal and the Ministry of the Sacrament come as its close and climax—see the present author's suggestions on p. 60 of *The Paradox of Worship* (SPCK, 1977).

6

Holy Communion: The Service

In this chapter, we shall follow the pattern of Rite A, but will include comments where appropriate on the corresponding parts of BCP or Rite B.

At the beginning

Celebrant, server, and choir need to be recollected before the service begins. If a worshipful atmosphere is to be created, bustle must be stilled for at least a few moments. See p. 55 above for comments on preparation of priest and server. A useful vestry prayer is the Collect of Trinity 6 (BCP; in the ASB, the last Sunday after Pentecost, p. 745).

Choir and celebrant should enter through the congregation. To use a separate east end entrance makes it look as if they are actors on a stage rather than the representatives of the congregation performing certain liturgical actions on behalf of the rest.

The vessels are out of the way on the credence table. No acknowledgement should be made of them at this point. We are about to begin the Liturgy of the Word; the Liturgy of the Supper comes later. If there is to be any 'solemn entry' at this stage, it should be the Bible which is the subject of it.

After the initial greeting between president and people (mandatory in Rite A, permissive in Rite B) the first fixed item is the Collect. In ASB, therefore, the possibilities of variation at the opening stages of the service are manifold.

The chief matter for choice in Rite A is whether the penitential section should be at the beginning (sections 5–8) or after the intercessions (25–28). If we have it early, we emphasise that before we do anything else, we should recognise our sinfulness and our unworthiness to offer worship to God. (Some people will be moved by the ecumenical argument that the penitential section is at this point in the Roman rite.) To use the act of penitence after the intercessions makes a different point. It allows us to listen to the Word, respond to it in Creed and intercessions, and then make a formal recognition of the failings both of ourselves and the world for which we have prayed, before we begin the Eucharistic action.

When that decision has been taken, it should be easy to structure the rest of the introduction. What is important is not to over-load it. The first part of the service is the proclamation of God's Word. We should subordinate all else to this, so it is not helpful to use too many of the permitted options before the Collect. Let us show that we are eager to hear the Word as soon as we may!

With that *caveat* in mind, there are plenty of possibilities. Examples are: the introductory sentence at the back of the church, followed by a hymn or introit or *Venite* or *Gloria in Excelsis* or *Kyries* (according to season), during which the procession and the Book move to their respective positions; the priest from his place then makes the greeting 'The Lord be with you' or 'The Lord is here', and the Collect follows. Or the greeting may be made from the back of the church followed by the Collect for Purity as a preparatory devotion, then the *Venite* or *Kyries* or *Gloria* as processional, and the Collect on arrival at the crossing. Or a processional hymn on entry, followed by the greeting, Collect for Purity or *Kyries* or *Gloria*, then the Collect of the Day. And there are other options.

Note that if *Gloria* is sung, it is permissible (note 5, page 33) to use the 1662 words within an ASB service. Unless the congregation has the words in front of it, this will inhibit it from joining in, so bear this in mind, unless you are trying to emulate Cathedral practice and actually *want* a mute congregation.

If using 1662, it is best to say the opening Lord's Prayer in a quieter voice. It is really part of the priest's private preparation (the Amen is in Roman type, not italic) and the people's Our Father comes much later. The 1662 Collect for the Queen is usually omitted, as she is prayed for in the intercessions.

Ten Commandments or Summary of the Law. These may come here in Rite A unless the penitential section follows the intercessions. In either case, the commandments or summary are a way into the confession in which we acknowledge how far we have fallen short of God's commandments. In Rite B the Commandments are an introduction to the Ministry of the Word—as in BCP, a kind of invariant Old Testament lesson preceding the Epistle. When the prayers of penitence come near the start of Rite A, the Commandments perform both functions at the same time.

BCP has the commandments in full. Rite B abbreviates them. Rite A indicates the abbreviations by brackets, but also gives a form in which each commandment is glossed by a New Testament quotation (pp. 161–4).

There is much to be said for using the Decalogue at least on the first Sundays of Advent and Lent, and on Ash Wednesday. We may feel that it is negative and redolent of Old Testament legalism, but we neglect its basic morality at our peril.

Invitation, Confession, Absolution. After the invitation to confession, there should be a long enough pause for the priest (and congregation, who will have been standing hitherto) to get down to their knees before continuing.

The BCP (which, of course, does not have the Confession at this early point in the rite) prints three exhortations before the Invitation. They are almost never heard nowadays. The second of them, for use when the minister 'shall see the people negligent to come to the Holy Communion' merely scolds and is justly unused, but the others could well be heard more often. The first, which is to be used beforehand in giving notice of the Communion, calls us to self-examination and repentance, and could be used on Palm Sunday as a preparation for Easter Communion or on Quinquagesima in readiness for Shrove Tuesday and Lent. The third exhortation is a lead-in to the 'Ye that do truly'. Provided the reference to 'divers diseases, and sundry kinds of death' is omitted, there is no reason why it should not be used on occasion, as, for example, on the First Sunday in Advent.

The Collect. The Collect of the Day (which should be said standing, unless it has been immediately preceded by the Confession and Absolution) is the invariable part of the Preparation. On the use and choice of collects, see pages 36–38 above.

The Ministry of the Word

Lections. There may be two or three readings. Now the Family Eucharist has all but totally eclipsed Mattins as the chief Sunday morning service, we need to ensure that the Old Testament gets a fair look-in. If there are three readings, it is read every week. Otherwise (see note 10 on p. 116) the asterisked reading in the Lectionary on pp. 1049 ff. is to be used and becomes the 'controlling reading'. This means that the Old Testament lesson takes precedence over the Epistle in the nine Sundays before Christmas, and the opposite is the case during the Pentecost season.

ASB provides two psalms (or portions of psalmody) each Sunday, for use as introit and gradual. Note the rubrics at sections 14 and 16 in Rite A (9 and 11 in Rite B). Between Old Testament and Epistle only a psalm is permitted, as a transition from the Old to the New Testaments, but between Epistle and Gospel there may be a psalm, or canticle, or hymn. Note 8 on page 116 (Rite A) and note 3 on page 177 (Rite B) says that *Gloria in Excelsis* may be used here, but any of the Morning or Evening Prayer canticles are possible, so there is great scope for variety, even without going to the hymn book. If we use Rite A and have *Venite* at section 1, a psalm at 14, and the *Benedictus* or *Te Deum* at 16, the service is becoming very much like Morning Prayer. This is deliberate. Morning Prayer (and, less easily, Evening Prayer) and Rite A may be combined into a single service—see the ASB, p. 71. The rite can be shortened to ante-communion for those occasions on which a non-sacramental service is needed, by taking the service as far as the absolution (at its later position in the rite) and then adding Our Father, the General Thanksgiving and/or other prayers, and the Grace (see note 24 on p. 118).

If the readings are separated by psalms, canticles, or hymns, these ought to be subordinated to the lessons and related to them. They are all part of the Ministry of the Word and should not be treated as a musical relaxation during which the mind may safely be allowed to wander.

The choice of Bible translation for the lessons is governed by the Versions of the Bible Measure 1965; for details, see p. 33 above.

Dramatic possibilities for the readings include the traditional sharing of the Passion readings amongst several voices (see the book *Lent, Holy Week, Easter* (1986), pp. 142–175), miming, acting out, or the use of slides or pictures if the church is accustomed to using an overhead projector; and a Gospel Procession is a means of adding visual honour to the climax of the Ministry of the Word.

This can be done simply by the celebrant moving as close as possible to the people, or with full ceremonial honour. In the latter case, details of what to do may be found in *The Celebration of the Eucharist* by Hugh Moore *et al.* (Church Union, 1975 but still in print and as apposite to ASB as it was for Series 3), pp. 6f.

Sermon. Since the sermon in ASB follows immediately upon the Gospel, it is appropriate for the gospeller to be the preacher and for the Gospel to be read from the pulpit in order to prevent an undramatic pause in the flow of the service. If the gospeller is not the preacher and there is a Gospel Procession, the preacher ought to go to the pulpit during the gradual in order not to snarl up the procession.

The linking of Gospel and sermon means that liturgical preaching is to be encouraged. According to R. H. Fuller of the American Episcopal Church (*What is Liturgical Preaching?*, SCM Press 1957, p. 22),

> the purpose of the sermon is to extract from the scripture readings the essential core and content of the gospel, to penetrate behind the day's pericope to the proclamation of the central act of God in Christ which it contains, in order that the central act of God can be made the material for recital in the prayer of thanksgiving.

Professor Fuller has put the whole Church in his debt by a succession of books in which this ideal is worked out in practice. His *Preaching the Lectionary* (Liturgical Press, available in the UK through Columba Press, Dublin) can be adapted without difficulty to the ASB readings on most Sundays.

It is worth drawing attention to the importance of the sermon. In both ASB rites, the section number of the sermon is printed in black as an invariant part of the service, not in blue as if it were optional, and the prefatory note (12 to A, 5 to B) states that the sermon is an integral part of the Ministry of the Word and should normally be

preached at *all* celebrations on Sundays and other Holy
Days (our italics, but the point is firm).

Creed. The Creed may be omitted except on Sundays
and Holy Days. It is the declaration of a community,
hence the 'We believe' of Rite A in place of the 'I believe'
of the other rites. It has been traditional to face east to say
the Creed—not towards the altar but towards the rising
sun, as we proclaim Christ the Sun of Righteousness.
Nevertheless, if there is a central altar, it makes more
sense to continue to face inwards rather than to turn to
face east.

Notices. In Rite B, the notices may come immediately
after the Creed and before the intercessions. This order is
also allowed in Rite A (note 19, p. 117). In BCP, sermon
and offertory are interposed. The Rite B order enables
notices and prayers, liturgy and life, to be much more
closely related. Even if the notices are given out at the
beginning or end of the service, or made available in
duplicated form, it is proper at this point to mention such
of the notices as tie up with the intercessions which are to
follow. The people can then be given news of an invalid,
or informed about forthcoming events, in preparation for
praying about them. That lessens the danger of such
incongruities as 'We thank you, Lord, that Josiah Bloggs
is now well enough to sit up and eat a little dry toast', or
'We thank you, Lord, that the Sale of Work raised £250
after all the expenses were paid, although there are still
some amounts of money to come in'. On the notices in
general, see above, pp. 22–23.

Offerings. In Rite A (by authority of note 20 on p. 117)
the offerings of the people may be collected at this point,
though if they are, they are not to be presented until
section 24, at the Preparation of the Gifts. In Rite B, they
may be presented as well as collected here—presumably
to cover the words in section 17 where mention may be
made of 'alms and oblations'. This is not to be encour-

aged. To present the alms here and the elements later makes a dichotomy between our gifts of money and the gifts which are the objects of the Eucharistic action. Many churches nowadays have no collection of alms, but a bowl at the entrance.

Intercessions and thanksgivings

The intercessions are preceded by an invitation to prayer. If possible, persuade your congregation to remain standing for this, then (if it is the practice in your church for them to kneel for the intercessions) allow enough time for them to do so before continuing. Otherwise, all but the first few words of the invitation will be said inaudibly as the congregation noisily get to their knees.

Distinguish carefully between biddings and interces-sions. A bidding is a request to the congregation before the prayer begins, and is in the form 'let us pray for . . .'. Intercessions are addressed to God, within the prayer, in the form 'we pray to thee/you for . . .'. Once the bidding is over, the interceding begins and it is not proper to revert to biddings within the body of the prayer. Nor is it proper to mix 'thee' and 'you' language. If the prayer is in the 'thee' form, so should the biddings be, as well as the extempore intercessions within it.

When BCP is used, an alteration in the order may be helpful. The rite prescribes the order: notices, sermon, offertory sentence, offertory, biddings, intercessions. If the biddings are moved so that they come immediately before the offertory sentence, the congregation have opportunity to make the subjects of the biddings into their own prayers whilst the offertory is taking place. This is particularly useful when the biddings take up the message of the sermon.

The scope of the intercessions varies in the different rites. BCP's is for the Church alone, and within it only for that part which is militant here in earth. Rite B's is for 'the whole Church of God in Christ Jesus, and for all men according to their needs'. Rite A allows us not only to pray for Church and world, but also to thank God for his goodness. Thanksgivings need to be sparing at this point in the service. Here, primarily, we are interceding. It is the Eucharistic Prayer which is the Great Thanksgiving. In particular, thanksgiving for the kerygmatic events of our redemption are included specifically within the Eucharistic Prayer and so are not necessary at this point in the service.

In all the new rites, versicles, responses, and free prayer are optional. The prayer may be said as a continuous whole without interspersing it with other material, or the free prayer may precede the complete set prayer, or be used at only some of the possible points. Five sessions of extempore prayer may be too many, unless the leader is very self-disciplined as to their length.

The intercessions of ASB are designed to be the prayers of all the faithful, not just those of the celebrant. Practical suggestions about achieving this (and reasons why it is good to do so) may be found in the present author's *The Paradox of Worship* (SPCK, 1977), pp. 56–7.

In the 1662 prayer for the Church Militant, and in the Rite B First Intercession (section 17), the words 'to accept our alms and oblations, and' are to be omitted 'if there be no alms or oblations'. This covers an ante-communion without a collection. If there is a communion without a collection, simply omit the words 'alms and', since there will be Eucharistic oblations to offer.

Movement. If the intercessions are said from the nave (as they nowadays commonly are) and the prayers of penitence are at sections 24–28, immediately following the intercessions, how is the priest to move from the body of the kirk to be ready to face the people at the absolution? To do so during the confession itself is not seemly— does he not also need to confess *his* sins? If the intercessions are led by a lay person there is no problem. If there are two priests, the one who leads the intercessions may move back to his position in choir or sanctuary during or after the Peace. If one priest is doing the service solo, the best solution is to move after the intercessions, in silence, and begin the invitation to confession (or Decalogue or Summary of the Law) thereafter.

Humble Access. The Prayer of Humble Access has a firm place in the devotions of English churchpeople. So have the Comfortable Words, but neither of these were happily placed in BCP, and ASB has not entirely solved the problem.

Rite B puts this prayer as an option between absolution and Peace, but it obtrudes between the declaration that we are put right by God and the Peace in which we are affirmed as the Body of Christ. In Rite A, if the prayers of penitence come early, the Prayer of Humble Access (or its fine but neglected alternative in section 82) comes between the intercessions and the Peace, looking rather as though the revisers needed to put it in somewhere but could not for the life of them think of a suitable place. If, on the other hand, the prayers of penitence come at their later position, the Prayer of Humble Access comes as it does in Rite B—a word of assurance, as if the absolution was not assurance enough, and breaking the link between absolution and the Peace.

The Gordian solution is to omit the Prayer of Humble Access altogether, but if it is so loved that to do so would cause scandal in a congregation, remember that there are worse sins than an occasional attack of liturgical impropriety.

The Peace. The words are mandatory, the action permissive. When we celebrate the fact that we form one Body, we need to be aware of each other. The Peace therefore should be said standing, with eyes open. Kneeling with head in hands is highly inappropriate.

Rite A provides seasonal variants for the words of the Peace (section 83) which are worth using.

Whether anything more happens than the spoken formula, will depend on the congregation and its leaders. Continental hugs put many people off. It is probably best to be completely and naturally English, and use a straight handshake, with or without the formal words. If the Peace is passed, it should fan out from the President, to symbolise that God's peace comes from his altar.

The Peace is the most natural place at which to bring the children back if they have been having their instruction separately. Where this happens it is also possible to allow the formal liturgical action to stop for a few moments whilst the children find their families and the adults greet each other informally. This is not an intrusion into the liturgy but the point at which the words about being one Body and one fellowship are translated into action. This is especially useful if there is no Church Hall, or if people are unwilling or unable to stay for coffee in the church building after the service is over.

If the children are meeting separately during the first half of the service, can their leaders afford regularly to miss the Ministry of the Word? It may be possible for the priest or one of the parish staff to say the first half of the service with the leaders either in a side-chapel or where the children meet, beforehand. In this way the children's leaders do not suffer from that starvation of the Word which might be the case if they customarily only came into church for the Ministry of the Sacrament.

The Ministry of the Sacrament

The Preparation of the Gifts. Whether or not they have been collected at a different point in the service (though see pp. 65–6 above), this is the point at which the offerings of the people ought to be presented. 1662 has a rubric which sadly has not found its way into the ASB: the priest 'shall humbly present and place it upon the holy Table'. The offerings of the people are not a part of the meal, but they are properly placed on the same table as the bread and wine, even if momentarily, before being handed back to the server.

An infelicity of ASB is that it requires the bread and wine to be placed upon the table before the offerings of the people are presented and before the sidesman can give the communicant numbers to the priest. Some churches overcome this problem by having a kind of 'score-board' at the west end of the church carrying the numbers for the priest to see. There needs to be an understanding as to whether these numbers include the sanctuary party or not. To avoid all doubtfulness, it is best to give the congregational number followed by the sanctuary number—for example '45 plus 2'. If the ASB order is reversed, the sidesmen can whisper the number when they present the alms, and that prevents the need for a supplementary dip into the bread-box after the numbers are known.

Alternatively, there may be a ciborium at the west end in which intending communicants place a wafer as they enter. If so, the celebrant would do well to add one or two extra from the credence, as people often forget their drill as they come in.

Many churches have an 'offertory procession' through the nave with the Eucharistic elements. This has been condemned as Pelagian, but need not be so. We can offer God nothing but what he has already first given us, and the sentence provided for use at the offering of the alms drives this point home. (So do the 'appropriate words' often used at section 33 when thanking God for his gifts of bread and wine—'*through your goodness*' we have bread and wine to offer.)

Note that in Rite A the bread and wine 'are placed' on the table (passive voice) but the president 'takes the bread and cup into his hands' (section 36, now the active voice). This shows that it is the liturgy of the deacon (or assistant or server) to 'lay the table', but the presidential part of the liturgy is to perform the four Eucharistic acts of which the first is the 'taking'. In silence, the priest lifts the chalice and paten/ciborium off the table for a few seconds, thereby signifying the bread and the wine which are to be the object of the rest of the Eucharistic action. In Rite B (as in BCP) the 'taking' is done as part of the manual acts within the Eucharistic Prayer itself.

Bread and wine. Canon B 17 states that 'the bread, whether leavened or unleavened, shall be of the best and purest wheat flour that conveniently may be gotten, and the wine the fermented juice of the grape, good and wholesome'.

It is not easy to reconcile the Breaking of the Bread and the words about 'because we all share in one bread' with the use of separate wafers. If there is resistance to the use of ordinary leavened bread, it is at least possible to have unleavened oblong wafers which break into a dozen or so pieces. If leavened bread is used, it may be wise to score a piece beforehand so that it breaks easily without forming too many crumbs. The best is a small bridge roll or bread bun with a soft crust, which can be broken into almost any number of fragments whatever the size of the congregation.

If there has been trouble with alcoholism it is possible to obtain fermented grape juice from which all but a negligible percentage of the alcohol has been chemically removed. Such wine is sometimes used in Methodist churches, and the local Communion Stewards of the Methodist Church would be able to put you in touch with local suppliers.

A little water is customarily added to the wine. In our Lord's time (see 2 Maccabees 15.39) wine was never drunk without an admixture of water.

The Eucharistic Prayer. What BCP called the Prayer of Consecration is in Rite B called the Thanksgiving and in Rite A the Eucharistic Prayer. The change is deliberate. What consecrates is not a verbal formula, still less the manual acts at a certain part of the prayer, but the whole

Eucharistic action of the assembled People of God. There are, therefore, no prescribed manual acts in Rite A, and, although note 16 on p. 117 allows them, it is far more consonant with the theology of the rite as a whole not to use them. If he wishes to, the president can lay his hands on the bread and cup (or stretch his hands over them) at the traditional moments; or (better) mark off the words of institution by making the sign of the Cross at the words 'grant that by the power of your Holy Spirit these gifts of bread and wine may be to us his body and his blood' and again at 'we celebrate with this bread and this cup'.

An elevation of the bread and cup is in order at the very end of the Eucharistic Prayer. Remember that such actions, if done, need to be seen by the people—a broad sweep, not a fiddly gesture visible only to the servers. Similarly, if the priest bows or genuflects, he should remain in position for a second or two so that the gesture may be seen from a distance to be significant.

The Thanksgiving from *Sursum Corda* to doxology or final 'Amen' is (to quote note 3 on p. 115) 'a single prayer, the unity of which may be obscured by changes of posture in the course of it'. The appropriate posture for praise and thanksgiving is to stand, but so many congregations insist on dropping to their knees immediately the *Sanctus* and *Benedictus* are over that it is probably a lost cause to try and teach them better.

As to choice of Eucharistic Prayer, users of the ASB are offered an *embarras de richesse*. Rite B has two. The first derives from 1928 via Series 1, and the second from Series 2. The choice will largely depend on how conservative of language and expression the congregation wish to be. In Rite A there are four possibilities (plus the 'Order following the pattern of the BCP'), and all were hammered out by the synodical Revision Committee with the experience of Series 3 and the debates on that rite as a background. It would be a travesty to say that the first is a 'general purposes' prayer, the second for Evangelicals, the third for Catholics, and the fourth for those who still retain a sneaking regard for the BCP, but there is some evidence that, crudely speaking, that is how the use of the rite has worked out in practice. Each prayer has its own distinctive emphasis. The first is based on the celebration of the one perfect sacrifice. The second is controlled by the idea of 'memorial'. The third has its roots in a third-century Eucharistic prayer of St Hippolytus, whilst the fourth is closer to the wording of the BCP. What is important, however, is that synodical representatives of all theological persuasions within the Church of England, in the debates on Rite A, expressed themselves doctrinally satisfied with all the Eucharistic Prayers in that rite, so that no one prayer can be regarded as wearing a party badge. Some churches have shown the splendour of their impartiality by using all four in rota on the four Sundays of the month (and the 'Order following the pattern of the BCP on the fifth').

Whichever prayer is used, it is a courtesy to the congregation to say at the outset, e.g., 'the first Thanksgiving', or 'the third Eucharistic Prayer', so that everyone can follow the whole of it in their books.

All the rites have proper prefaces (33 of them in Rite A, though the final three of them are suitable only for the fourth Eucharistic Prayer or the order following the BCP pattern). The Maundy Thursday proper is also suitable for the Thursday after Trinity Sunday (Corpus Christi) and on other occasions of special thanksgiving for the institution of the Eucharist. In Rite B, there are separate sections of prefaces for the two Thanksgiving Prayers. Note that all the prefaces are addressed to God the Father, except in the BCP form of the Trinity Sunday preface. This is addressed to the whole Trinity, so the words 'Holy Father' in the common preface have then to be omitted.

The Rite A acclamations ('Christ has died . . .') are optional—see note 15 on p. 117, which also allows them, if used, to be prefaced by 'Let us proclaim the mystery of faith', or other suitable words.

Some churches, hoping to involve the whole congregation in the Eucharistic Prayer, have the people join in saying its final paragraph or paragraphs. This is not to be encouraged. Each part of the whole Body has its own liturgy, and this part is the President's liturgy. There are plenty of places within the rite where the people may legitimately exercise their liturgy; this is not one of them. They make the President's prayer their own by their 'Amen' (1 Cor. 14.16).

The breaking of the bread. If the people have not dropped to their knees half way through the Eucharistic Prayer, they should kneel at the 'Our Father', before the breaking of the bread. The breaking is one of the four Eucharistic actions and ought to be seen by the people as significant. If unleavened bread is being used, there should be a large wafer which can be broken in full sight of the people. When the bread is leavened, the breaking can be made to take some time as it is divided into the appropriate number of portions.

The giving of the bread and cup. If the sacrament is to be reserved for the sick, this will be done before the communion of the people. The reserved sacrament is taken out of the aumbry (it will be consumed by the priest either immediately after his own communion or at the ablutions) and replaced by the requisite number of freshly-consecrated breads which—if the sacrament is to be reserved in both kinds—have been touched, via a piece of the priest's wafer, with a drop of wine from the chalice. The reserved sacrament is normally replaced once a week at least.

Before the distribution (Rite A, section 45) the priest invites the congregation to draw near and partake. This formula is obligatory in Rite A, and its position is important. It comes before the priest's communion—there is no justification for separating the communion of the priest from that of the people by the words of invitation. (The priest may, if he wishes, communicate last instead of first.) The people need to be instructed to take this formula of invitation literally, and to begin drawing near with faith as soon as it has been spoken, so that they are in position and ready to receive by the time the altar party has communicated. Otherwise they hang back, there is a hiatus in the service, and the invitatory formula loses its point.

Since 1559 the Church of England has used an inclusive formula at the administration which combines the words of 1549 ('The Body of our Lord Jesus Christ . . .') and those of 1552 ('Take and eat this in remembrance . . .'). It is important that both are used. To give simply the first half is to destroy the balance of Anglican Eucharistic theology and to reduce Anglican comprehensiveness to a narrow form of 1549 doctrine. Since, therefore, the formulae in section 46 of Rite A are of a 1549 type, the invitation with its 1552 emphasis is essential to counterbalance them. Rite B makes similar provision by requiring either section 38 with its combination of 1549 and 1552, or section 39 with a 1552 invitation and 1549 words of administration.

In the BCP rite, the minister will probably want to spread the words of administration over three or four communicants unless the congregation is very small. It is better to stress the words in the manner '*for* thee' rather than 'for *thee*': the former emphasis is on the theology of the atonement, the latter makes the reception too individualistic.

If stamped hosts are used, it is very little extra trouble to ensure that they are put into the communicants' palms the right way up for them to see the emblem properly.

With today's mobile population, habits of communicating in any one church are likely to vary considerably, and every minister should be prepared to administer according to the wishes of the communicant, even if he does not like the theology implied in some methods of reception. When using the BCP, the rubric forbids the placing of a wafer directly into the mouth, but the ASB contains no such prohibition. When a parent brings a babe in arms, it may be a great help to place the bread direct into the mouth.

Unconfirmed children often come to the altar rail for a

blessing. There should be some prearranged signal to show which they are, so there is no danger of doubt, mistakes, or questionings. Either ask them to keep their hands and heads down, or ask them to carry a prayer book. If there is more than one minister, they do not receive more than one blessing. In a small congregation where all the names are known, the children appreciate being blessed by name. If the minister is anxious about having a lapse of memory or using the wrong name, it is better not to try.

When delivering the bread or the cup, allow the communicant time to say 'Amen' before receiving. If there are two ministers, the one with the wine should ensure two or three communicants' space between them so that the communicant has had time to consume the bread before he is offered the wine. With three ministers, one with bread and two with wine, it is better for those with the wine each to communicate alternate people rather than taking half a rail each.

Communion may be received either standing or kneeling. When there is a large number of communicants it can be quicker (and no less seemly) to have one minister with the bread and one with the cup and for the communicants to file up to the one, receive standing, and pass on to the other. Since it takes longer to receive the cup than the bread, it is even better to have one minister with the bread and one either side of him with a cup each, and to direct the communicants alternately left and right. When administering to standing communicants it is necessary to hand them the chalice for them to deal with it themselves, and it will in practice be found necessary to consecrate more wine than when the same number of people communicate and the administrant holds the chalice.

In some places, there is an attempt to emphasise the togetherness of the congregation and the priesthood of all believers by having them pass the chalice and paten from person to person. It is doubtful if this achieves much by way of speed, symbolism, or seemliness.

There has been much discussion in recent years about the hygiene of the common cup. Infection is minimised by the alcohol in the wine and the metal of the cup (glazed ceramic chalices are almost as effective, unglazed ones much less so), but it is still wise to wash the vessels in very hot water after each service. Little is achieved by using a purificator after each communicant, though this may have its value in reducing anxiety, and the administrant should always carry a purificator when communicating the people, to wipe off the lipstick which some thoughtless members of the congregation wear. If the people can see that the minister rotates the cup a little between communicants, this also helps to put some fears at rest. Those with heavy colds or infections can be advised to keep the bread in their hands and dip it in the wine (the method known as 'intinction'). Some people use intinction to avoid catching any stray infection, but the clergy, who have to consume the remains after the whole congregation have used the cup, seem to survive despite it. Guidelines put out by the Archbishops during the early days of the AIDS scare in 1987 reinforce the medical advice that there is no danger in the common cup, but precautions may allay anxiety.

Post-communion

The ablutions may be taken either immediately after the communion (ASB) or after the final blessing (BCP). They need not be performed in the sight of the people. BCP requires them to be done by 'the priest' (i.e. the celebrant) and anyone he calls to him; the ASB does not specify whose job it is. The assistant ministers can perform this task either at the credence or in a side-chapel. 'After the service' (Rite A, section 49) is a phrase of wide interpretation. It usually means 'during the final hymn', not 'after the congregation has all gone home'.

The communion of the people is the climax of the service. Liturgically, and dramatically, as little as possible should happen thereafter. One fault of BCP is the length of its post-communion material. ASB makes nothing mandatory except a post-communion prayer and the dismissal. Think very carefully before adding any of the permissive material. Does it overload a part of the service which should be brief and to the point? The post-communion sentence (with the ASB readings on pp. 403 ff.) is a useful way of finishing the service with a reminder of its seasonal significance, and many congregations have grown to love the use of *both* the Rite A post-communion prayers (sections 52 and 53). Technically, the blessing is unnecessary, as the communicants have already received the greatest blessing this world affords by taking the sacrament into their bodies, but the seasonal blessings of the ASB are much used and liked, and to deny them to the people smacks of that kind of doctrinal and liturgical pedantry which offends far more people than it pleases.

What *is* to be deprecated is that tendency to prolong the post-communion by recessional hymns after the dismissal and by 'vestry prayers' said at the back of the church for the benefit of the congregation. The rubrics (section 50 in Rite A, section 43 in Rite B) make it quite clear that the hymn is intended to follow the post-communion sentence (and cover the ablutions) and *precede* the final prayer(s), blessing, and dismissal. It is possible to do otherwise under cover of note 20 on p. 117 which says that 'if occasion requires [the hymns] may occur elsewhere', but if there is a blessing, the dismissal should be said from the altar, and there is nothing left to do then but depart. If there is no blessing, there may be a recessional hymn after the post-communion prayer, and the dismissal may be spoken by the celebrant (or deacon, despite the rubric) from the west end of the nave after the hymn and whilst the people are still standing. If the people are then loath to leave the Lord's Table (which is to their credit) they should be left to stay with their own devotions and not made to take part in a vestry prayer. Vestry prayers, as their name implies, are to be said in the vestry as private devotions for servers and choir, who do not have the same opportunity as the rest of the congregation for remaining in their places for their private parting devotions.

Vestry prayers may include the Collect of Thanksgiving for the Institution of the Holy Communion (ASB p. 920) or the BCP collects of Trinity 6 or 7 (ASB collects of the Last Sunday after Pentecost, and Pentecost 17), or a collect from those printed at the end of the BCP Communion rite (ASB pp. 105 ff.). The prayer 'May the souls of the faithful, through the mercy of God, rest in peace' is offensive to some people for the reasons spelt out in the Doctrine Commission's report *Prayer and the Departed* (SPCK, 1971). It may be replaced by the prayer in that report, which has become section 13 of the ASB Funeral Service (p. 315): 'May God in his infinite love and mercy bring the whole Church, living and departed in the Lord Jesus, to a joyful resurrection and the fulfilment of his eternal kingdom'. That prayer, as the Commission said, 'only asks for such things as we are scripturally persuaded are in accordance with God's will and have not already been granted' (Report, p. 51).

7

Occasional Offices

Thanksgiving after birth

It is doubtful whether the 1662 form of 'Thanksgiving of women after child-birth, commonly called the Churching of Women' is nowadays used anywhere. It is designed as a private devotion in the church building, for the mother and the priest only, and speaks of 'the great danger of child-birth'. ASB provides two services—one of thanksgiving for the birth of a child and one of thanksgiving after adoption—and expects (note 3, p. 212) the whole family to be present, and for these services to be combined with Morning or Evening Prayer or the Holy Communion, though (note 5) they may be used on their own, in which case the minister is free to add hymns, scripture readings, and a sermon.

'Churching' as such is rarely requested (even in the north of England, where the custom lingered longest); but those who dislike what they call 'indiscriminate' baptism and wish to offer parents, instead, a service of thanksgiving, have it here. It includes prayers for the child (section 7, p. 215; section 14, p. 217) though they fall short of being an act of infant 'dedication'. The minister must (note 2, p. 212) explain that this service is not a baptism. If the service is used within the Eucharist, it follows the sermon and may replace the intercession (unless it is placed at the very beginning of the rite).

Baptism

ASB makes it clear that the baptism and confirmation of adults is the liturgical norm, and infant baptism comes well down the list of available services. Nevertheless, in most places the baptism of infants is more usual than that of adults, so we will deal with it first.

The minister. Baptism is properly performed by the priest, and, in his absence, by a deacon or deaconess. The Canons do not include baptism in the duties of a lay worker. If, however, the child is in danger of death, baptism may be administered by any person—lay or ordained, man or woman, orthodox or heretic, Christian or not—so long as water is used and is poured over the child with the words, 'I baptise you in the name of the Father, and of the Son, and of the Holy Spirit (or Ghost). Amen.' The name is not necessary so long as the identity of the person baptised can be duly recorded. The person who performs the emergency baptism should also add the Lord's prayer and a blessing (see p. 280 of the ASB for suitable wording), though if this is omitted, the baptism is not, of course, invalidated. The baptism must be entered in the parish register (see p. 24 above).

If the child lives, he should be brought to church and 'received into the congregation' by the priest or deacon, who will use the normal baptismal service with the exception of sections 17 and 20 (52 and 55) and with modified words at section 18 (53). If it is not certain that water and the name of the Trinity were used at the earlier ceremony, or when it is not certain that a person has been baptised, the words to use (ASB p. 270) are, '*N*, if you have not already been baptised, I baptise you . . .'.

Who may be baptised? See Canons B 22 and B 23. Parishioners have the right of baptism and the minister may not refuse or delay, providing due notice (normally a week) has been given and the provisions about godparents have been observed. The only legitimate reason for delay is to give time for preparing or instructing parents, guardians, or godparents. A minister wishing to baptise a child whose parents are not resident in his parish or on its electoral roll must first seek the goodwill of their own parish priest, but if he withholds his goodwill, the parents' parish priest cannot forbid them to have their child baptised elsewhere. Any minister baptising a child in hospital or on a sickbed must enter the baptism in the parish register of the place of baptism and send the name and address of the child to the parish priest where the child's parents live, unless they are on his own electoral roll.

Adult baptisms should be preceded by instruction, prayer, and fasting, and notice of them should be given to the bishop or his nominee for that purpose at least a week beforehand (Canon B 24). Normally adults will only be baptised if they are about to be confirmed. There is no justification for baptising an adult who does not want to go on to confirmation (even if he wants a visa for entry to an Arab country and needs to prove that he is a Christian). Children who have 'missed out' on baptism are best left unbaptised until it is time for their confirmation, unless (see ASB p. 225, note 2) there is to be a baptism of a whole family. It is best to combine adult baptism with confirmation, but if it is found embarrassing to the candidate, a semi-private baptism may be performed beforehand.

Choice of service. BCP, Series 2, and ASB are currently authorised (see p. 3 above). The decision rests with the minister, but any of the persons concerned has the right of prior objection. If agreement cannot be reached, the bishop's ruling is final.

When should baptisms take place? Canon B 21 says that 'it is desirable that' baptism should normally be administered 'on Sundays at public worship when the most number of people come together'. This clearly is meant to discourage a virtually private service attended only by the child and its family. It is the Church into which the child is being baptised, and if the Church is not represented, the service denies in action what it says in word. This is especially noticeable in ASB—in section 53 the parents and godparents are told they must 'declare before God and his Church' the faith in which the child is to be baptised, and in section 38 the priest and people together welcome the newly-baptised into the Lord's family as fellow-members of the Body of Christ. Nevertheless, if there are so many baptisms in a particular parish that it would be a constant disruption of regular Sunday worship to insist that all baptisms are carried out at the Parish Eucharist, then use Sunday afternoons as a second-best. Normally, however, a public baptism at a regular service once a month or once a quarter is not out of the question, though it may have to be a 'mass baptism' rather than an individualised service. If it is well organised (and if the provisions of the ASB on p. 250 are observed) it will not greatly add to the length of the worship. The baptism service comes immediately after the sermon, and the Eucharist is resumed afterwards at the Peace. The sermon is often omitted as a way of further abbreviation. At Morning or Evening Prayer, the baptism comes after the second lesson.

The font. A custom has grown up in some churches of having a small portable font placed at the east end of the nave for baptisms, since a font at the west end is thought to be inconvenient and the pews are not designed for turning right-about-face in. There is, however, still much to be said for the traditional position, which symbolises by the placing of font, chancel step, and altar the Christian's progress from baptism through confirmation to the Holy Communion. Altar and font should stand in separate and distinctive places in the building, each emphasising its own special purpose and teaching as equally significant Gospel sacraments. There is no harm at all in having the people turn round in their pews for the baptism (which is not the whole of the service—see below). Canon F 1 states that the font should stand as near to the principal entrance of the church as conveniently may be, and should be set in as spacious and well-ordered surroundings as possible. The Canon also states that the font bowl shall be used for no other purpose whatsoever than for the water at the administration of holy baptism. It should *never* be used for floral decorations—it is a font, not a flower-vase.

Before the service. Fill the ewer with water (warmed, if necessary, as a concession to the frailty of the flesh) and place a shell or scoop with one or two clean purificators at the edge of the font. It is important to put people at their ease. Rehearsal is not necessary, though some priests like it. Best is that blend of informality with dignity which comes with practice—neither backslapping bonhomie nor frozen rectitude, but making the participants feel welcomed. Have the service in a book or on a card, but still tell people as the service progresses, what sections to say and what are being omitted; ask them to join in the congregational prayers, and do not leave everything to depend on their intelligent reading of the rubrics which will be more familiar to you than to them. When addressing the sponsors, look at them, and when addressing the congregation, turn yourself round to look at *them*. It is possible to adopt a louder voice for speaking to the congregation without making the words to the sponsors inaudible to the rest of those present. Speak slowly and clearly; make it obvious that you have got time to be bothered with the words of the service; above all, know what you are going to do, and where, how, and when you are going to move. Your confidence will rub off on to the nervous godparents, who will afterwards be surprised how much they enjoyed the service.

The geography of the service. BCP tells the priest to come to the font at the very beginning of the service and then to fill it with pure water. ASB allows him to take the opening part of the service where he will, and only instructs him to stand 'before the water of baptism' at section 52, when the water is blessed. It is better to ignore the 1662 rubric when using the BCP service. Make a procession to the font after the questions and prayers for the candidates: priest, godparents, parents with candidates, and any small children who want a good view. Be friendly and informal; formality and solemnity are not synonymous. Arrange the party near the font, then fill it publicly from the ewer and you are ready to bless the water.

The signing with the cross and the giving of the candle are ceremonies associated with baptism. If the signing is done at the font with the baptismal water, confusion between the signing and the baptism can only be made more likely. ASB allows the signing to take place either before or after the actual baptism (sections 49 or 56) and to be done either dry or with oil specially blessed for the purpose (usually by the bishop on Maundy Thursday)— see note 3 on p. 241.

A good practice is to complete the baptism at the font, then take the child (followed by parents and godparents) to the altar. There he can be signed (dry or with oil) and be handed his candle which is lit either from the altar candle or (preferably) from the Paschal Candle standing nearby. (Have a taper ready, to transfer the light.) Priest and congregation then welcome the newly-baptised (section 58) after which the baptismal party return to their seats and the service continues.

Baptism is not a naming ceremony. BCP has the words 'Name this child' but ASB assumes that the child already has a name and allows it to be used well before the moment of baptism. An additional Christian name may be taken, or an existing one changed, at confirmation (see below, pp. 86–7), but not at baptism.

The baptism. The baptism may be performed by immersion (unlikely) or by sprinkling. It ought not to be done by smearing the child's head with the priest's wet thumb. Use a shell or scoop, and put the water on the child's head so that it trickles over him, then wipe it dry with the purificator you have put ready at the font's edge. The water may either be poured once at the words 'I baptise you', or (preferably—see p. 242, note 9) three times as the name of the Trinity is pronounced, 'testifying to the faith of the Trinity in which candidates are baptised'.

Confirmation

Confirmation is the bishop's service (see p. 9 above) and it is for him to say what rite is to be used, and to agree the liturgical details with the incumbent. BCP has a single rite; ASB provides orders for the baptism and confirmation of adults, the baptism of families and confirmation of adults, and the confirmation of those already baptised. Any of these may be used on its own, at Morning or Evening Prayer, or with Holy Communion. The custom of integrating confirmation with the Parish Eucharist on the Sunday of an episcopal visit is growing in popularity, though it could not become the norm unless there were to be far fewer confirmations or unless

> Bishops in their shovel hats
> Were plentiful as tabby cats

which is unlikely. But if you want your confirmation in this way, ask your bishop.

Many dioceses have standard instructions about the arrangements for, and conduct of, the service. The clergyman concerned should ask the bishop (or his secretary or his chaplain). In case of doubt, the advice of a Rural Dean or neighbouring incumbent is worth seeking; it will be tailored to local conditions, peculiarities, and personalities.

A candidate may alter his or her Christian name, or add another one, at the time of Confirmation. Halsbury's *Laws of England* (Vol. 14, *Ecclesiastical Law*, 4th edition, 1975, paragraph 1000, note 1) states that 'when this is desired, the bishop, in his prayer at the laying on of hands, mentions the person by the new or altered name, and at the conclusion of the rite signs a certificate of his having confirmed the person by that name, the effect of which is afterwards noted in the register of the person's baptism. It is also noted in the register of confirmations.'

Reception into the Church of England

Unbaptised members of other churches are admitted into the Church of England by baptism. Those who have been baptised but not episcopally confirmed are received by confirmation. Those who have been baptised and episcopally confirmed either by the laying on of hands or anointing (in practice, Roman Catholics and Orthodox) are received by the use of a special form of words. Each diocese has its own regulations. The form of words is either one issued by the bishop for that purpose, or the (very simple) form agreed by the General Synod. The bishop should always be consulted beforehand, as he needs to give his permission for the reception. If the person to be received is in priest's orders, he can be received only by the bishop or his appointed commissary. Lay people are customarily received by their parish priest. See Canon B 28 for details.

Institutions, inductions, visitations

The form of institution (or collation) and induction of an incumbent or the licensing of a priest-in-charge is issued on the authority of the Ordinary, and he will be in charge of the liturgical arrangements. Similarly, if the archdeacon wishes to hold a visitation in your church for the swearing-in of churchwardens and the delivery of the Charge, he will be in touch with you about the details.

Marriage

There is good pastoral and legal advice in *A Handbook of Parish Work* by Michael Hocking (Mowbrays, revised edition, 1984). Here, we deal mainly with the liturgical aspects of the service and its preliminaries.

Who may be married in church? The service is intended for couples at least one of whom is either resident in, or on the electoral roll of, the parish, though this requirement may be waived by the authority of the Archbishop of Canterbury's Special Licence. In law, parishioners have the right of marriage in their parish church even if neither of them has been baptised, though theologically it makes a mockery of a Christian sacrament to use it for non-Christian participants. If either partner has been divorced and has a former partner still alive, the clergyman has a legal right to marry them if he wishes, any episcopal ruling to the contrary notwithstanding. If he does not so wish, he can neither be legally forced to perform the ceremony nor to allow his church to be used for that purpose by any other person. (Nullity is not divorce; consult your bishop's legal secretary if in doubt.)

Each diocese has its recommendations about the remarriage of divorcees which carry moral authority but have no force in law. The situation is fluid, so consult your bishop for up-to-date and local advice. Services of prayer and dedication for use after civil marriage have been provided by the Liturgical Commission, approved by the General Synod, and commended for use by the House of Bishops (see p. 4 above).

Banns. Banns should be read out with the notices at the morning service. They may only be read in the evening if there has been no morning service. They should be read three times, on three Sundays (not necessarily consecutive). They remain in force for three months after the third publication. The formula is either that in the first rubric of the BCP marriage service or the ASB one at note 1 on p. 285. It includes the words 'This is the first (etc.)

time of asking'; *not*, please, '*for* the first time'. It does not include descriptions such as 'bachelor', 'widow', etc; if it is necessary to call banns for persons who have been divorced, there is therefore no need publicly to mention the fact. Whatever his disapproval of remarriage after divorce, the clergyman may not refuse to call banns for such a purpose.

After calling the banns, it is always appreciated if the minister either commends the couple concerned to the prayers of the congregation, or offers a prayer there and then for them. If there is to be a prayer, let it be a short one.

Choice of service. BCP, Series 1, or ASB (see p. 9 above). Within ASB there are two possible forms of vow—sections 11 and 12, the latter with the bride 'obeying' her husband. Either section 11 or section 12 has to be taken as a whole; note 6 on p. 285 points out that an eclectic mix of the two is not permitted. The priest should enquire beforehand which form the couple prefer. They have the right of objection to the form chosen by the priest, but the choice should be a mutual one when discussing the wedding arrangements. ASB, on pp. 301 ff., shows how to combine the Eucharist with a wedding. Sadly, not even practising members of Christian congregations always want it.

The minister. The ministers of the sacrament are the couple themselves. The clergyman is there to give the Church's blessing and to register the ceremony for the purposes of the State. As the service involves a blessing, the officiant is normally a priest (and in what follows, we shall for simplicity's sake assume that this is so), but marriages performed by deacons are just as valid.

Before the service. A rehearsal a day or two beforehand helps the bride and groom to be as much at ease as possible on their great day. It is also a good opportunity of explaining to them the service and its Christian implications.

The service is not going to be taken casually by the bride and groom (to say nothing of the bride's mother). What may seem a chore to the officiating priest is the day of a lifetime for the couple. He owes it to them, therefore, to ensure that the church is clean and tidy (and the vestry also) and that he has a freshly-laundered surplice. He will wear a white stole; if the church has one, a cope is appropriate.

The priest arrives fifteen minutes early to welcome the groom, best man, and groomsmen, to collect the fees and to make sure the registers are properly made out (and checked by the groom in person). There should be no last-minute instructions to the participants, only a calm confidence that the priest is in charge and nobody need worry about the details of the service.

Five minutes before time, the groom and best man go to their places, whilst the priest moves to the west door, ready to welcome the bridal party. When she has arrived and is ready, the priest precedes the bride down the aisle. This makes sure the procession goes at the right speed and is a courtesy to the bridal party. Remember, however, that the guests want to see the bride, not the priest. Ask her (and her father) to ensure that there is a clear gap between yourself and her as you move down the aisle.

The service. The bride comes down the aisle on her father's arm, to the chancel step, whilst the groom comes out to meet her there. His best man is a pace behind him and a pace to his right. The bride hands her bouquet and gloves to the chief bridesmaid and we are ready to begin. (We follow ASB; modifications for BCP or Series 1 are easy to make.)

Sections 1–5 are optional. If there is no sermon at 5, it may be delivered at section 22. The service will probably begin better if (with or without an opening hymn at the bride's entry) the priest starts off with a brief word of welcome to the couple and the congregation, says where in the service book the order of service is to be found, and then launches straight into the introduction (section 6). The words 'The vows you are about to take . . .' (section 8) should be said in a quiet voice to the couple, but the questions beginning '*N*, will you take *N* to be your wife?' should be spoken firmly and clearly as if you *meant* the whole congregation to hear them. Before the first question, a whispered 'Be ready to say "I will" ' to the groom is reassuring; it need not be repeated to the bride. The question is a long and complicated one and the couple may not remember exactly when it is coming to its end. To prevent them from answering before they should, it is useful to arrange at the rehearsal that the priest will read the question from the book and only raise his eyes to the groom or bride when the time comes for them to make the response.

In these liberated days, the 'giving away' of the bride is optional (see note 5 on p. 285), and ASB has omitted the question 'Who giveth this woman to be married to this man?' which caused so many brides' fathers in the days of the BCP to make unscheduled answers. If the tradition of 'giving away' is retained, then the bride's father takes her right hand in his right hand and places it in the priest's right hand; he in turn places it in the right hand of the groom, who keeps it there whilst he makes his vow to his bride. At this stage, since the couple are marrying each other, let them turn inwards and face each other rather than looking towards the priest. After the man has made his vow, the couple loose hands and the woman takes the man's hand (same hand, but the loosing and taking signify that the action is freely entered into on both sides) to make her vow. They then loose hands again and the priest turns to the best man with his prayer book open so that he can place the ring(s) on it.

If the hands are hot and the rings will not go on easily, do not force them. Leave the wearer to ease the recalcitrant object over the knuckle at a convenient later stage.

The priest then declares the couple to be husband and

wife, and joins their right hands together. Some priests like to tie the stole round the joined hands in token that the union is blessed by Holy Church. Otherwise, let the priest hold his own hand round the couple's clasped hands as he says 'That which God has joined together . . .'. He would then be wise to say 'The congregation remaining standing, let us pray', and then whisper to the couple, 'please kneel'. The priest then blesses them (section 19) and the acclamations may then follow.

The registers may be signed now or at the end of the service, and there is a scripture reading (the choice is free, but the Eucharistic propers on pp. 302–4 provide a good quarry) and the sermon. The best man and bridesmaids go back to their seats in the nave and the congregation is bidden to sit. The bride and groom remain standing in front of the priest. Clearly, the sermon should not be a long one. Five minutes is an absolute upper time limit. A whispered tête-à-tête with the bride and groom simply gives rise to ribald speculation as to the nature of the advice the priest is giving them. The sermon should be for the whole congregation to hear, and should declare what Christian marriage is about.

The priest then whispers to the couple 'Follow me to the altar rail', announces the psalm or hymn, and turns to go to the altar. The remaining prayers are said as the couple kneel together at the rail. After the final prayer and blessing, unless the registers have been signed at an earlier stage in the service, the priest leads the newly-weds to the vestry for the registration.

If (as is desirable but unusual) there is to be a nuptial mass, the order of service is laid down on page 301 of ASB.

Registers. Registers need to be signed by priest, bride, groom, and at least two witnesses. It helps to ensure smooth running if the number of signatures is kept to the minimum and the witnesses have been chosen before-hand. The registers may be signed in full view of the congregation immediately after the marriage and before the psalm (section 21), but it is more usual to lead the party into the vestry for the signing after the whole proceedings are over, so that the final procession may lead out from there. The exit may be headed by a verger bearing his rod; the priest should at this stage stay out of the picture until the party has left the building. His last act should be to hand the bride her 'marriage lines', marshal the procession, and send it off.

Sickness and healing

BCP's Visitation of the Sick has for long been a dead letter, and the revised provisions were not ready by the time ASB was published in 1980. As a result, the new rites are in a separate publication *Ministry to the Sick 1983* (also known as ASB 70). This includes forms of Rite A and Rite B Communion for use with the sick, forms of laying on of hands with prayer, anointing, commendation of the dying, and prayers fo use with the sick.

Communion of the Sick. If the patient is in hospital the chaplain will arrange for him to receive the Sacrament, though it is helpful to let the chaplain know that he has a communicant in his unit.

Communion of the sick at home can use either the whole service, or it can be from the reserved sacrament. The former may be appreciated, but care must be taken not to tire the patient with too long a service. It is important that the patient should know beforehand exactly what to expect, especially if this is the first time he has received his Communion in this way, and does not know about intinction or realise that he may be communicated in one kind only. He may otherwise be worried about the omission of the Eucharistic Prayer, or at the brevity of the service.

Relatives could be asked to prepare a table in the sick room, with a white cloth, cross and candlesticks (if available) and flowers. Some parishes have sick communion sets with all necessary items, and a group of lay helpers can be responsible for their care, distribution, and collection after the service. But these are optional. Often the priest will have simply to come to the bedside and improvise, and this is no bad thing. Our Lord does not wait upon ceremony.

Let friends and neighbours and members of the congregation come if they are invited, and receive their communion with the sick person.

It is good to have a book or card with the whole of the rite on it, especially if it can be left beforehand with the patient. Card ASB 71 contains the form of the distribution of Holy Communion at home as well as forms for the laying on of hands and anointing. Rite A for use at home or in hospital is on card as ASB 73, and Rite B as ASB 74. Remember, however, that older patients may prefer 1662 even if their church has used the ASB for many years past. This is a time for the pastoral care of the patient, not for our own liturgical preferences or idiosyncrasies.

Healing services. There is no form of service put out by authority, so the minister is free to use services of his own devising or to use and/or adapt material put out by other groups. Sound advice may be had from the Acorn Christian Healing Trust at Whitehill Chase, High Street, Bordon, Hants GU35 OAP.

The recommendations of an Archbishops' Commission of 1958 in its report *The Church's Ministry of Healing* are still relevant, as is shown by the fact that an abbreviated version of the report was published in 1987 (as *The Church's Healing Ministry*, prepared by John Richards and published by Marshall-Pickering and Renewal Servicing). The Commission recommended that:

1. The Church's ministry of healing should always be closely related to its normal and regular worship and pastoral work. The ministry to the sick people of his parish and congregation is a regular part of the parish

priest's ordinary work. Where a healing service takes place he should normally conduct it himself and undertake both the preparation and subsequent care of those who attend.

2. It is desirable that when possible there should be a celebration of Holy Communion when the laying on of hands or Holy Unction is given in Church, so as to make clear that the ministry of healing is closely related to the saving work of Christ and the strengthening and life-giving power which he gives to the members of his Body in this Sacrament. The objectivity of the Church's worship in Holy Communion is, moreover, a salutary corrective to the subjective and emotional tone which can easily become dominant in healing services.

3. At healing services only those should be ministered to who are known to the parish priest or to the conductor of the service if he is not the parish priest, and who have been prepared in advance. The presence of relatives, friends and intercessors is to be welcomed. Care should be taken to see that all present understand the purpose of the service. (Unabridged report, para. 118, pp. 54f.)

The practice of encouraging people to come to healing services without preparation and follow-up is to be deprecated. As the Commission said (para. 116(e), page 54):

When a number of persons are ministered to without preparation and with no subsequent pastoral care, there is clearly a danger that they may be gravely depressed if there is no apparent result of the kind for which they hoped. Their plight will usually be unknown to the minister or, if known, may be beyond his skill to alleviate. The medical treatment of such persons is likely to be made more difficult and additional harm is caused if, as often happens, they attribute their failure to get better to their lack of faith.

The warning has often been repeated but is not always heeded.

The Commission believed that the practice of advertising healing services was undesirable, and recommended that ministers of other denominations, or laymen, should not take part in a healing service in a parish church without the bishop's permission. This may sound restrictive, but to observe it is rarely burdensome and may prevent things going badly wrong.

The ministry of deliverance. Exorcism is the direct command in the name of Christ to an evil spirit to depart from a person who (or a place which) has become possessed by it. It is not the same as a prayer to God that the sufferer may be delivered from evil or an evil spirit, nor is it the same as the offering of the Holy Communion in a disturbed house with the special intention for the repose of the soul of a person (known by name or unknown) who is causing psychic disturbances there. Neither exorcisms nor this kind of a Requiem Eucharist should be undertaken without expert guidance. Every diocesan bishop has his adviser, or team of advisers, in this ministry to whom to refer cases. Healing services should not include exorcism. The stringent requirements announced by the House of Bishops at General Synod in 1975 forbid exorcism as a public ministry. If practised:

1. it should be done in collaboration with the resources of medicine;
2. it should be done in the context of prayer and sacrament;
3. it should be done with a minimum of publicity;
4. it should be done by experienced persons authorised by the diocesan bishop;
5. it should be followed up by continuing pastoral care.

The Christian Exorcism Study Group (re-named the Christian Deliverance Study Group with effect from 1987) put out a report entitled *Deliverance* (edited by Michael Perry, SPCK, 1987) of which Appendix IV consists of twenty pages of liturgical and prayer material. Much of this derives from a draft report of the Liturgical Committee of the Church of the Province of South Africa. It contains forms for the blessing of a house (with or without Holy Communion), the rite of exorcism of a home or other place, form for the blessing of holy water, a rite of deliverance (or minor exorcism), and prayers and devotions for private or liturgical use. The rite of major exorcism was not given, as it should only be used on rare occasions by competent persons under the direction of the diocesan bishop.

Holy Unction. The anointing of the sick is a scriptural practice (see Mark 6.13, Jas 5.14f). In the ancient Church there were many such anointings or unctions—at baptism, confirmation, ordination, and coronation. The final one in the series was the anointing of the sick, which therefore became known as the last or extreme unction. Later practice associated this with imminent death, but there is no reason why this should be so. In Anglican use it has been a rite which may be repeated, as a rite of healing not as a rite specifically of preparation for death. Nevertheless, it is well not to give unction to a person too frequently, but to make it a kind of 'once per illness' rite, to be used only after special pastoral preparation.

The form of service is that in ASB 70 or ASB 71 (see above p. 93). The oil should be pure olive oil blessed by the bishop—usually at the Maundy Thursday Eucharist ('Chrism Mass') at which the propers from ASB pp. 555–7 are used. If episcopally-blessed oil is not available, the priest may bless his own, using the form of words in ASB 70.

Unction is best administered just before the blessing at the Eucharist, though (especially if the patient is very ill) it may be given on its own apart from any other service. The priest will have the blessed oil in a small silver vessel, a little cotton wool and/or breadcrumbs to help remove the oil from his fingers, a purificator or towel, and a lavabo bowl of water.

The sign of the cross is made in oil on the person's forehead, using the celebrant's right thumb and the words of administration. The priest then cleanses his own hands with the cotton wool, breadcrumbs and water, and continues with the rest of the rite. Afterwards, the cotton wool and bread is burnt and the contents of the lavabo bowl poured into the church piscina. If desired, the rite may be amplified with readings and intercessions. ASB 70 gives a proper Collect, Epistle, and Gospel.

Funeral rites

The law. A body must not be disposed of until a registrar's certificate or a coroner's order has been issued. The service is normally taken by the priest or deacon but with the goodwill of the person(s) responsible and at the invitation of the incumbent the service may be read by such deaconesses or lay workers as have the bishop's authorisation to do so (Canons D 1 and E 7). Burials normally take place in consecrated ground and a minister cannot be compelled to perform any part of the burial service on unconsecrated ground. Conversely, neither can he be censured for doing so, unless he used a service which, had it been performed on consecrated ground, would have been inappropriate. If he *does* bury in unconsecrated ground, Canon B 38 requires him to bless the grave beforehand. A suitable prayer is to be found at the end of the 1928 burial order; it was not included in ASB.

Authorised rites are BCP, Series 1, and ASB (see p. 3 above).

A rubric preceding the BCP rite says that this service is not to be used over unbaptised persons or suicides. There is no such rubric in ASB, and indeed its services were designed so as to be usable in the case of suicides. Strictly, as the service is Christian burial, and the unbaptised have not been received into the Christian Church, it is inappropriate to bury the unbaptised with Christian rites.

Wise pastors will leave questions about the baptismal status of the deceased unasked when they are making funeral arrangements, unless the deceased was known to be an adherent of a non-Christian religion or openly and specifically antagonistic to Christianity.

Canon B 38 declares that cremation is lawful in connection with Christian burial and that in such case the service may be held either in church or at the crematorium. No incumbent is under any legal obligation to perform a funeral service within the grounds of any burial authority, and if for any reason the incumbent refuses to take the service at the crematorium, the person having charge of the crematorium may ask any other clergyman to do so. Provided he has the bishop's permission to officiate, that other clergyman is at liberty to accept the invitation if he wishes to, without consulting the incumbent. The crematorium authorities are under no legal obligation to ask either the incumbent of the parish in which the crematorium lies, or the incumbent of the deceased's home parish, to perform the service. The courtesies of good practice have to be built up locally.

Save for good and sufficient reason, the ashes should be interred or deposited, by a minister, in consecrated ground. The scattering of ashes is not to be encouraged (see Canon B 38). For registers, see p. 24 above.

The rites. BCP is a simple, if structureless, rite. Series 1 is a considerable improvement, and ASB makes provision for various eventualities—the burial of a child, prayers after the birth of a still-born child or the death of a neonate, for cremation, for the interment of ashes, for a service which may be used before a funeral either at home or when the body is brought into church the night before, and for the celebration of the Eucharist in connection with a funeral. There is a wide selection of sentences, psalms, lessons, and additional prayers. ASB also has Eucharistic propers for commemorating the faithful departed on 2 November or on any other suitable occasion (pp. 834–7).

Before the funeral. There can be a service at home before the body is taken away, or in the church if the body is to lie there overnight. There may be a celebration of the Holy Communion either the night before or on the morning of the funeral or at the funeral itself. This is only suitable for a regular communicant and, even so, many people doubt whether it is appropriate to make the funeral itself (which will probably be attended by many non-communicants) a Eucharistic occasion.

The funeral service. It is much to be desired that at least some part of the service take place in church, even if the interment or cremation is to be conducted under local authority auspices. In towns, this often involves united action by all the clergy, and united representations to the undertakers; but it is worth insisting that a person's body should be taken into the church before we say goodbye to it. The conduct of the service is more controllable in church than in a crematorium chapel, where it is all too common to find saccharine sentimentality, piped background music, and Handel's *Largo* all combining to create an air of unreality which seeks to minimise the stark finality of death. In church it is easier to confront people with a religion which helps us face the real world of pain and death rather than with something which tries to insulate us from its impact.

The officiant wears a surplice and black (or white) stole, or surplice with scarf, bands, and hood. Meet the corpse and party at the lychgate or church door. Try to be solemn without over-formality. The opening sentences may be said either in procession on the way from the lychgate, or they may be begun as the priest enters the church door, or (best) the procession enters in silence or to the organ accompaniment, so that the sentences can be said when all are in place, listening, and ready to begin.

The burial or cremation may precede the service in church. If so, the cremation can be a day or two before the service, so that the funeral service can be combined with the interment of the ashes.

A memorial service. There is no form of memorial service as such provided by ASB, but sections 1–11 (pp. 307–14) provide a useful base around which one can easily be constructed. Alternatively, so would the Holy Communion service with the ASB burial propers or the propers of All Souls' Day (pp. 834–7). There will be hymns and an address. The latter should be a declaration of the gospel of the resurrection, not merely a panegyric biography of the deceased.

8

Through the Year

Advent

An Advent carol service should have for its theme the preparation for Christ's coming; it ought not to be simply a Christmas carol service held a month early. The service can have as its theme 'from darkness to light' and begin in complete darkness, save for the taper held by the priest who reads the bidding prayer. The choir's tapers are lit from this for their first item and the lights in the church are put on for the first congregational hymn. If the church is big enough, the choir can move during the course of the service in procession from west to east. The prophetic lessons are read whilst the choir is in the nave and the Gospel replaces the Prophets when it reaches the sanctuary. Suitable lections for a service of six readings and carols are: Isa. 40. 3–11; Mal. 3. 1–5; Isa. 35. 1–10; Isa. 11. 1–9; Luke 1. 26–38; and Luke 4. 16–21.

Christingle

A Christingle consists of an orange which symbolises the globe, wound round with a piece of red ribbon (the blood of Christ) and speared with cocktail-sticks carrying pieces of dried fruit (the fruits of the earth). The whole is surmounted by a candle (Christ the Light of the World).

Children who come to make their gifts are given a Christ-ingle in return, which they light at the close of the service, which is generally held some time during December. Instructions as to how to make Christingles, leaflets about their history and significance, and forms of service are available from the Church of England Children's Society, Edward Rudolf House, Margery Street, London WC1X 0JL.

The Christmas tree

Though of pagan origin, the tree is now so much a part of our Christmas that it ought to be baptised into the Christian celebration. Those who are unhappy at anticipating Christmas during Advent may compromise with popular demand by lighting the tree ceremonially in church on the fourth Sunday in Advent, reserving the blessing of the crib for Christmas Eve. The church is in darkness except for the altar candles. A child bearing a taper lights it from these and goes to the tree at the west end of the church to light a candle on the tree. As this is done the electric tree lights are simultaneously switched on. Texts such as Isa. 9.2, Ps. 27.1, Ps. 4.7 (PBV), Jn 1. 4–9, Jn 8.12, and 1 Jn 1. 5–7 can be incorporated either as proclamations or as versicles and responses. Children leave their gifts at the foot of the tree during or after the ceremony.

The crib

The crib is made ready beforehand, but the figure of the Christ-child is not placed in it until the crib is blessed, on Christmas Eve. The shepherds remain in the crib until the Epiphany, when they are replaced by the Magi. The crib is taken away on the Octave of the Epiphany. For suitable prayers of dedication, see the books recommended on p. 41 above.

Christmas carol services

There are many permutations and combinations of lessons for the Christmas carol service. A fairly 'traditional' set is Gen. 2. 5–9; Gen. 3. 8–13, 23–24; Isa. 9. 2,6,7; Isa. 11. 1–9; Luke 1. 26–33, 38; Luke 2. 1–7; Luke 2. 8–20; Matt. 2. 1–11; and John 1. 1–14. *Magnificat* is appropriately sung either to a congregational chant or a choral setting immediately after the lesson of the Annunciation.

The Bible Society, Stonehill Green, Westlea, Swindon, Wilts, SN5 7DG, publishes an attractive full-colour folded leaflet with the full text (Good News Bible) of nine readings under the title *The Saviour is Born*. The readings are Isa. 9. 2–7; Micah 5. 2–5a; Luke 1. 26–38; Matt. 1. 18–24; Luke 2. 1–7; Matt. 2. 1–12; Luke 2. 8–20; John 1. 1–14, and Hebrews 1. 1–3.

New Year

Anglicans could well take a leaf out of the Methodists' book and adapt their Covenant Service for use at the beginning of the secular New Year. It is a serious service for serious Christians and recalls them to their duty towards God. As published in a traditional language version in the 1936 Methodist Book of Offices, or as revised in modern language in 1974 and available in a leaflet published by the Methodist Publishing House, it is designed as the main service of the day for the first Sunday of the year and includes sermon and Lord's Supper. It is easily adapted and abbreviated for use with Anglican rites or in other liturgical contexts.

6 February

Forms of service for the anniversary of the Queen's accession are appended to BCP. There is no ASB provision. At Mattins or Evensong, there are proper psalms, lessons, and suffrages after the Creed, a special collect to follow the collect of the day, and prayers for use in place of the State Prayers. If 6 February is a Sunday, the propers of the Sunday are to be used at the Holy Communion, with the collect of 6 February following it. If it falls on a weekday there are proper lections, and the collect replaces that of the day. In addition, there is a brief service for use at any time of day, consisting of the *Te Deum* and some prayers.

Lent, Holy Week, and Easter

Anglican liturgical provision between Ash Wednesday and Easter is now likely to be dominated by the book *Lent, Holy Week, and Easter* (Church House Publishing, Cambridge University Press, and SPCK, 1986), hereafter referred to as LHWE. The forms of service in it have been commended by the House of Bishops. Any bishop may authorise the forms within it for use in his diocese, or authorise a special diocesan adaptation of them, or authorise quite different services. If the diocesan bishop gives no direction, the priest is free to make whatever use of the services he wishes, so long as he observes Canon B 5 in reverence, seemliness, and sound doctrine. It must be stressed that LHWE is a directory from which choices may be made, not a straitjacket. Use of its provisions in any parish or situation requires 'selectivity, sensitivity, and imagination'. Some priests and congregations will wish to supplement LHWE either from Roman Catholic sources, or from the work of the Joint Liturgical Group (*Holy Week Services*, SPCK and Epworth Press, 1971), or from their own resources.

All the points made in Chapter 2 above need to be reiterated. The congregation must be prepared for the innovations of these services, and, when they are put together, care and rehearsal will be needed so that what happens is what is intended to happen, not a shambles of bumbling inefficiency. In particular, the notes at the beginning of each of the services of LHWE should be carefully read and pondered as the parish observances are being planned and rehearsed. If that is done, then the enrichment of our worship at these seasons will enable us to enter into the experience of the central events of our redemption in a new and potentially life-changing way, which is one of the aims of all Christian worship.

Ash Wednesday. LHWE has an *Order for the Beginning of Lent* within a Eucharistic framework. A special introduction explains to the worshippers the meaning of Lent and invites them to observe the season faithfully. There is a penitential litany and a form for the imposition of the ashes made by burning the last year's Palm Sunday crosses. There are also two non-Eucharistic services of penitence.

Mothering Sunday. There is no special provision in LHWE for the fourth Sunday in Lent, but many churches will wish to keep it as Mothering Sunday and to encourage families to attend. The Children's Society (Edward Rudolf House, Margery Street, London WC1X 0JL) produce special Mothering Sunday cards advertising their work.

Palm Sunday. LHWE points out that the procession with palms is the first of the commemorative liturgical actions of Holy Week, which reminds us of the main events of the last week of Jesus' ministry. The reading of the Passion Gospel on Palm Sunday takes us into the heart of Holy Week. The LHWE service therefore begins with a 'commemoration of the Lord's entry into Jerusalem' consisting of a blessing of palms and the reading of the Palm Sunday story, continues with a procession round the church with palm crosses or branches, and leads into the Eucharist at which the Passion Gospel is read and there is a special litany of intercession, in which we stand with Christ in his suffering.

Holy Week. Holy Week should be planned as a whole.

It is too easy to put on a series of unconnected services or devotions that make the whole week 'bitty' and unsatisfying. Not everybody will want (or be able) to come to everything, but the observance should be planned so that every item, though self-contained, is intelligently related to the whole. LHWE makes no special provision for the Monday to Wednesday in Holy Week. The Joint Liturgical Group offers outline services on the themes of penitence (Monday), obedience (Tuesday), and service (Wednesday). BCP provides Eucharistic propers in which the story of the passion is retold by Matthew (Sunday), Mark (Monday and Tuesday), Luke (Wednesday and Thursday), and John (Good Friday). Holy Week services should be an opportunity of telling once more

> the old, old story
> Of Jesus and his love

so that the faithful may enter more fully into the contemplation and sharing of his passion, and may desire to order their lives in the light of it.

Maundy Thursday. The Blessing of the Oils (ASB pp. 555–7) is the bishop's service and so is not included within LHWE. The Maundy Eucharist of LHWE includes a special intercession, a commemoration of the institution of the sacrament, and a ceremonial washing of the feet. A Maundy Watch may follow which (p. 179) 'should be observed at least for an hour, preferably until midnight, if not until the liturgy for Good Friday'. The altars are stripped and the lights extinguished either in the course of or at the end of the watch (see LHWE p. 180, note 6 for details). Unless the bread and wine are to be used on the following day, the aumbry is emptied, and not replenished until the first Eucharist of Easter Day.

Good Friday. The staple diet on Good Friday used to be the Three Hours' Devotion, but this is rapidly declining in popularity and being replaced by an hour at lunch-time or the setting-forth of the passion in the evening either at a

Eucharist or Office or an *ad hoc* service (often ecumenical in nature, in which case the form suggested on pp. 31–3 of the Joint Liturgical Group's book of *Holy Week Services*, and based on the ante-Communion, may be found acceptable).

If the Three Hours is kept, it may be done either as a service entirely planned by the conductor round a series of addresses (traditionally but by no means necessarily on the Seven Words from the Cross), or liturgically with Mattins, Ante-Communion and Veneration of the Cross, and Evensong.

A devotional service of nine lessons and hymns or chorales based on St Matthew's account of the Passion, with text by Richard Tatlock and music selected by Desmond Ratcliffe, is published by Novello (1973) under the title *The Passion of Christ*. Words for the use of the congregation are published separately.

Many parishes will, however, take advantage of LHWE to establish a new pattern of Good Friday worship. Opinion as to the propriety of celebrating the Eucharist on that day is changing. At one time, it was kept as a day of dereliction and desolation on which only the ante-communion could be contemplated. LHWE believes that 'on this, above all other days, it is wholly appropriate to eat the bread and drink the cup, thereby proclaiming the Lord's death until he comes'. A compromise is not to celebrate the Holy Communion on Good Friday but to give communion from the sacrament reserved from the Maundy Thursday service.

LHWE's Good Friday liturgy consists of four parts—the Ministry of the Word, the Proclamation of the Cross, the Intercessions, and the Holy Communion. The first and third of these are always to be used and correspond to the ASB ante-communion. The other two parts provide a dramatic and sacramental way in which we may 'look on him whom they pierced'.

Holy Saturday. There should be no celebration of the

Eucharist on this day. Evening Prayer is *not* to be treated as the first evensong of Easter, but as a eve or vigil. By tradition, Christ was born at night, so there is something proper about a Christmas midnight Eucharist; but the tomb was, we know, discovered empty at daybreak, so the Easter ceremonies belong, not to midnight on Easter Eve but to dawn on Easter Day.

Easter Day. LHWE divides the Easter liturgy into four parts. The Vigil is kept (in darkness, as much as may be) either throughout the whole night, or during a part of it, or at least as a brief prelude to the Service of Light, which is the second part of the ceremonies. At this, the Paschal Candle is lit. If each member of the congregation can light his candle (either directly or mediately) from the Paschal one, the dramatic symbolism of Christ, the light of the world, rising from the darkness of the grave, is immensely powerful.

The Paschal Candle is lit at all services between Easter and Ascension, to show that Lent and Holy Week are not an end in themselves but a preparation for the Great Forty Days of Eastertide. Thereafter the candle should be used at all baptisms, and may also be lit at funeral services.

The third part of the Easter liturgy consists of baptism (or, at least, of the renewal by the congregation of their baptismal vows). The 'natural and proper climax of the whole Easter liturgy' is the fourth part, the Holy Communion.

Many churches will have an Easter Garden. Forms of prayer in connection with this may be found in LHWE p. 277.

Rogation

Traditionally, the parish bounds were beaten at Rogationtide (the days between Easter 5 and Ascension Day). 1928 provided three prayers for use at this time—the harvest of the land, the harvest of the sea, and the harvest of industry. ASB (pp. 884 ff.) gives three different collects. One is that of Easter 5, one prays that in our work we may bring the resources of the world within reach of every creature, and one is for workers on the land. As Rogation is often close to May Day it would seem a suitable time for town parishes to have their 'Industrial Harvest Festival' at which, in place of fruit and flowers and agricultural impedimenta, the products of local factories could be displayed in church and prayers could be offered for the industrial life of the district and nation.

Remembrance Sunday

Forms of service were ecumenically agreed in 1968. The full text, with appropriate hymns, is given in a leaflet published by Eyre and Spottiswoode, OUP, CUP, and SPCK.

9

Services for Special-interest Groups

CHRIS NEWLANDS

There are many hazards awaiting those who would attempt 'Do it Yourself' liturgy. At the back of the church, on a dusty shelf, well out of sight, usually under the old prayer books with pages missing that no-one has had the heart to throw away, lie innumerable attempts at constructing special orders of service for that 'one-off' occasion.

The composer Handel, it has been said, knew a good tune when he wrote one—and indeed he wrote many. But having recognized the value of a particular tune, he did have the unfortunate habit of using it time and time again. Let us be charitable, and assume that the demands on the great man to produce a suite here, an opera there, left so little time, that he was forced to plagiarise himself.

The demands on the time of the parochial clergy are certainly no less stringent, and it is easy to see how an overstretched clergyman, having to come up with a special service for the St John Ambulance Brigade, could dredge up from the bottom drawer of his filing cabinet an order of service he constructed for the Brownies as a project when he was a curate in Borehamwood some 25 years ago. A nip here, a tuck there; a bit of filling here and hey presto—A Service of Thanksgiving! And who could tell? Unless the Commissioner for the St John Ambulance Brigade had been a Brownie in Borehamwood some 25 years ago.

This is not to say that every service for every group has to be entirely different. There are, of course, many features of groups and organisations which are held in common from the Brownies to the Venture Scouts, from the Young Wives to the Darby and Joan; but there are equally just as many different needs and expectations regarding the type of service which the occasion demands. What they need and what they expect may well be entirely different, and the handling of the service will require pastoral sensitivity as well as liturgical awareness.

Expectations will vary on the side of the groups or organisations concerned, depending (amongst other things) on how familiar their leaders are with church worship. Often, though not invariably, those who are less 'churched' will expect 'church' to be what it was like when they last went: whether that was to a christening, wedding, or funeral is immaterial. They will probably expect a 'hymn sandwich' followed by a sermon. ('Not too long, please, vicar. The children, you see, get so restless.') They will probably expect to be bored. From the minister's point of view, this expectation is a real gift, as any imaginative and lively suggestion is likely to be met with great enthusiasm. ('That sounds great, Vicar; I didn't think we could do that sort of thing in church.')

The hardest expectations to cope with are those which involve 'the way we did things last time' or, even more tricky, 'the way it has always been done'. One's predecessor is presented by the group as having been willing to do anything the group required, and as having little or no control over the direction of a service. There has to be exercised a gentle firmness which is not afraid to say a categorical 'no' when the expectations become too ludicrous, and the service degenerates into an excuse to get the flags out again—for pomp and ceremony *for their own sake*, and self-congratulation. It is always worth reminding people that when a group comes into church it is always *for God's sake* that they do so—whether to give thanks and praise to God for the past, or to commit themselves to the future; the centre of all worship in God's own house is the action of prayer and praise and thanksgiving to God.

Where then does a minister begin to construct an occasion worthy of the praise of God? And indeed, also worthy of the hard work and commitment which members of the concerned group have put in. At the time of writing this, I am involved in the preparation of an order of service for the Durham County Fire Brigade, to give thanks in Durham Cathedral for 40 years of service under the present administration. For people of such commitment, who daily are prepared to risk their lives for the sake of others, one must always be conscious that liturgical commonplace, platitudinous prayers, and patronising preaching have no place in the service of God when placed alongside such service and commitment to God's people. For a fireman, being poorly prepared to handle a fire would have disastrous consequences not only for himself, but also for the people he would hope to save. For a clergyman, being poorly prepared to take a service can also have disastrous consequences, though not with such immediate and tragic results. It can give the impression that the Church doesn't care—it can actively discourage people, and diminish what little faith some had before the Church began to interfere. For a clergyman to be poorly prepared is, regrettably, far too common an occurrence, so that people can with some justification accuse the clergy of being a bunch of well-meaning amateurs.

It is important, then, to bear in mind these two considerations when preparing an order of service for a special occasion:

(a) that the needs of the group concerned should be foremost at the time of preparation;

(b) that the service offered should be a worthy offering of praise to God, and worthy of the occasion.

To ensure an appropriate service, it is essential that the minister should know something about the group concerned; to visit, or attend a meeting is not only invaluable for discovering the right level at which to aim written prayers and sermon, but is the beginning of what could be a relationship which is fruitful for both church and organisation, even though it may not be the natural milieu of the individual. A fashionably pacifist young curate may find the idea of working with the Royal British Legion to be objectionable in theory—until he becomes involved with them, when he may be shocked to find that for many, their aims are surprisingly close to his own heart.

If there is someone in the group who is prepared to work with the minister in the preparation of the service, this is all to the good. But at all costs avoid committees in the preparation of services. Much time is wasted on irrelevancies, and if a committee is felt necessary, then let it meet solely to comment, it is to be hoped constructively, on what has been produced as a draft by the minister working with one, or possibly two others.

When the planning is completed, steps can be taken for the execution of the plan—both on the part of the organisation, and on the part of the church. Although some relaxed spontaneity is desirable, to take away from the excessively starchy formality which many will remember from coming to church in past generations, nothing is more destructive to an atmosphere and spirit of worship than the chaos which can come from a lack of preparation. If no-one seems to be in charge, those coming to worship will be tense and nervous—not open to the spirit of worship at all. If the leader is seen to be in command of the situation, they will relax, and be much more open, and ready to take in what is offered to them.

Written instructions may seem a chore, but they allow all those involved to know exactly what is to happen and when, and they are far more useful and effective than spoken ones. Although clergy and certain others are accustomed to leading acts of worship, the most unlikely people can go to pieces when asked to do what seems from a clerical point of view the most simple task. Having a black and white instruction sheet gives everyone the necessary confidence to do what they are supposed to with conviction, and do it well.

A printed order of service may seem like an unnecessary expense, but unless there are reliable duplicating facilities to hand, it is wise to be able to delegate the responsibility of producing an order of service to those who can do so professionally. Not the least of the benefits of having a printed order of service is the value of what a church presents to a congregation. An ink-smeared sheet of A4 with barely legible smudged typing may well be the other side of a PCC decision to give more money to the missionary work of the Church in India. This is, however, hardly to be read between the ink-blotched lines of what is supposed to be an order of service. And what about the missionary work of the Church in Britain? What importance are we seen to be giving to an offering of praise to almighty God when the take-home reminder of such a service is of a quality which no primary school teacher would allow for use by five-year-olds?

The printed order of service must be accurate, which will require careful proof-reading, for no printer is infallible. Misprints on the page can be a source of great glee in retrospect (a delightful howler spotted at proof in an order of service for a Carol Service in Durham Cathedral read 'The Shepherds go to the Manager'), but at the time they can destroy any atmosphere of worship as the bloomer is pointed out to neighbours who might have missed it, to right and left, pew before and pew behind. Then it must be ready in good time. There are many other less controllable worries to prey on the minister's nerves without the added worry of 'which is going to arrive at church first—the orders of service or the congregation?'

If the orders are ready in good time, it is always good to have a 'Working Copy' with all movements, instructions to readers, those leading intercessions etc. clearly written in the orders of service for those who need them. The leader should have a Master Copy, detailing all the movements, and those who are expected to play a part in the service should have a copy too.

In preparing for any act of worship, but especially worship with groups which will bring people into church who are not regular worshippers, we are engaged in evangelism. Each service of this kind is an opportunity to speak of God to those who have come freely to God's own house. What we present to them is of the utmost importance, and will be a crucial factor in whether or not they will return to church, or even feel comfortable coming to the minister at a future time of crisis.

And so we now come to the harder question of what to do, and what to say in a service with an organisation or group, and here I would suggest an ABC by way of a guideline of how we might proceed.

(A) It is important to be *A*ppropriate, remembering that many who come to church will know little or nothing about the Christian faith which we can so easily take for granted. Assume nothing regarding what people know about Christianity. People will resent a misplaced expectation of some scriptural knowledge, but again they do not take kindly to being patronised. A middle ground, although very hard to find, will win many friends.

(B) It is right to be *B*old in devising an order of service which is innovative and original. Set precedents if necessary, rather than following them. But however original the service is, the most important point is that it must . . .

(C) *C*ommunicate. We fail miserably in our task of leading worship if we do not bring people into communication with God, and with one another. It is the easiest thing in the world for the minister to do everything himself, to be 'up front' because his is the only voice which can be heard at the back. (If the minister's voice *is* the only one which can be heard at the back of the church, then that is the time to investigate the possibility of having an amplification system installed.) It is the minister's job to serve the people of God, and to lead worship. But this does not mean that the congregation have to watch the minister doing it. In a special service, too much input from one voice could very easily turn a potentially good act of worship into a monologue, which ultimately may not communicate effectively either with God, or his people. Participation by the congregation can have a transforming effect on the essence of an act of worship. Hymns, though the life-blood of participation, are not always enough. And a joining together for the final Amen after the minister's prayers and for the final Lord's Prayer does not always bring the people of God together in the act of worshipping him.

If there are printed orders of service, it is good to use this to full advantage by printing out some kind of litany with a congregational response. This could be anything, from the BCP or ASB litanies, to a specially written litany for the occasion, incorporating special intentions relevant to the occasion. In some cases this can be done very effectively with a musical setting using one of the 'Kyrie Litanies' from Jacques Berthier's excellent '*Music from Taizé*' (Collins) or Geoffrey Boulton-Smith's '*Music for the Mass*' (Geoffrey Chapman). When a musical setting is used for a special service, it is always useful to have a rehearsal with the congregation if time and the situation allow, and there are usually enough people who can read music to justify printing out at least the melody line of the music.

Working with groups can often seem like hard work, but the rewards can be worth all the extra effort when a special occasion eventually comes to bear fruit. The worship offered on an occasion when many people have come from far and wide to offer, through the medium of their group or organisation, prayers and praise and thanksgiving to God can be most uplifting for leader and congregation alike. It is not only our duty, but also our joy to enable groups as well as individuals to come together in his house, to sing his praise.

10

Family Worship
CHRIS NEWLANDS

There are many families which meet together in churches around the world to worship God—and yet all are one Family, with one Father. And just as in any human family, many often opposing needs are expressed at the same time. Within the family of one church, there is always the possibility that some members will not like the way that other members do things, and divisions will occur. Some will insist on Holy Communion according to the BCP at 8 a.m. and stoutly refuse to come to any of these modern services the Church has invented in the last sixty years. Some will come to the main Sunday service, regardless of what it is. Others will come to the Eucharist only when they have to—Christmas and Easter; and faithfully attend Mattins and Evensong whenever they are offered.

What a divided family most churches would seem to be if looked at carefully! The diversity is apparent for all to see, but there is little sign of unity even within one parish church! The idea of a Family Service—for the family of the church—could bring all these different factions together, or it could just create yet another faction. In most cases, it would seem that Family Services do not bring together all these parties which make up the family of a particular church. An additional service, designed to bring more people to church cannot be criticised, but what is its purpose? Why should there be a proliferation of services if people are not attending the present ones? The first concern may well be to look at the way the present services are organised and to try to isolate the reason people are staying away. Are the services lacking life, warmth, enthusiasm on the part of the leadership of the church? What do people come to church for; to receive information or entertainment, or to receive spiritual food, and fellowship within the Body of Christ?

Motives should be carefully scrutinised before bringing another service to the parish, and very great care must be taken in deciding how it might fit into the regular pattern of Sunday worship. If this is to be on a monthly basis, there is a temptation to supplant the main Eucharistic service with a non-Eucharistic model. The disturbance to the regular pattern is certain to be unpopular in many quarters (although that in itself is no reason to avoid change). If the service were to be in addition to the principal Eucharist, numbers for both would definitely suffer. When dealing with the facts and figures on paper, the obvious remedy might seem to be the choice of the lesser of two evils. But this black and white view does not bear in mind the pastoral needs of the individuals concerned, and an insensitive handling of people's needs in worship could only too easily lead to people finding alternative churches—either for that particular Sunday, or even for good.

Further to compound the question of the Family Service is the question of content. The position of the Eucharist as the central activity of Christians when they come together seems certain for the foreseeable future in most centres of Anglican worship. The reasons are twofold. First the Body of Christ in a particular place should gather round the Lord's table on the Lord's own day, to obey his command, and to find strength from doing so to be able to continue his work in the community. Secondly, and more practically, the structure of the service of Holy Communion is an excellent framework for the adoration of God; for receiving the assurance of sins forgiven; for receiving food for thought in the Ministry of the Word, and food for the soul in the Ministry of the Sacrament; for praying for ourselves and others; and for renewing our commitment to go out, refreshed and strengthened, ready to participate in God's work of re-creating the world according to his Word.

No Family Service which is aimed at a congregation where there is not necessarily the commitment of the Eucharistic family can attempt to be so wide-ranging in what is covered. The aim may be more evangelistic, appealing to people who are unfamiliar with church services—appealing to those as yet uncommitted, but sincerely questioning. Although there may always be a need for this type of service, it should not be seen as an alternative to the Eucharist, but an introduction to the Eucharist. The temporary perch must not become a permanent nest. The use of material from the Eucharist is in theory excellent, in that it familiarises people with the language of praise and thanksgiving. The *Kyries*, *Sursum Corda*, *Sanctus*, Acclamations, and even the *Gloria* can usefully be used in a context without the theological complexity of the Eucharistic prayers, and the action which for many is the hardest of all—to stand up and be counted among the Christians, by going to the altar rail.

For children, the process of growing up has been seen as leading towards confirmation, and rightly or wrongly in recent years confirmation has been seen as the ticket to receiving communion. But for adults, joining the Church unconfirmed may cause many problems where a visible decision has to be made, rather than just arriving at the right age, having been brought up in a Christian family, or a Christian school. There are often, however, those happy occasions when adults grow up in faith alongside their teenage children, and are confirmed together. This is, of course, a source of great joy for the church family, but the joy and strength which this can give to the family is boundless!

Having grown through the means of the Family Service

during this time of questioning and being nurtured in developing faith, there will be the strongest temptation to remain in this comfortable and familiar environment. But every effort must be made to welcome the newly confirmed as valued members of the Eucharistic family. This could be done by an act of welcome at the Eucharist the week after their confirmation, and allowing them to make an active contribution to that service, whether it is arranging the flowers beforehand, or reading a lesson; helping with an offertory procession, or helping to take the collection. The number of ways in which new members could contribute to the life of the church is vast, but it is probably wise to wait a little before inviting new members of the family to be on a subcommittee of the PCC in charge of boiler maintenance.

Regarding children in worship, much has been said in recent years to affirm the fact that they are as much a part of today's church as they are of tomorrow's. As baptised Christians, they are as much a part of the Church as any Christian up to and including bishops and archbishops. They have their needs, as do we all. They can also annoy other members of the Church, as can we all. The Church must nevertheless endeavour to do all it can to meet the requirements of all its members although this is rarely, if ever, possible. Children have a right to be in church, and other more senior members have a right to have a time of worship free from the interjections of the young who may not yet have learned that there is a time to express joy, and a time to be quiet. In some churches, a formula has been found, which has worked with reasonable success, whereby on one Sunday a month the principal morning service is given to a non-Eucharistic service aimed primarily at the young—a service which can attract large numbers of families with young children who are not regular worshippers. The traditional Evensong on these occasions gives way to a celebration of the Eucharist, which has a very different character to the morning celebrations, being rather quieter, and more reflective in mood.

The content of a Family Service need not follow a fixed form, but it is best to follow some skeleton which allows considerable room for additional material. A service where there is no sense of direction can be frustrating and embarrassing for all concerned, and this can be avoided by having a framework which shows clearly the direction of the service. A useful guide to remember is contained in the mnemonic ACTS:

Adoration	Praise and worship
Contrition	Confession and Absolution
Thanksgiving	Remembering all of God's goodness
Service	Commitment to follow God's way.

Organisations which work with children, and with which the church is linked, can be invaluable if they are encouraged to assist in the preparation of such services. Schools and uniformed groups are often more aware of the kind of level at which children are working than parish clergy; and if they are given enough notice, they can usually be relied upon to produce a very worthwhile offering at one month's service. They are also more likely to know the current top ten of children's hymns and religious songs, with which even the latest hymn books seem unable to keep up. Although the minister will doubtless have his own resources regarding hymns from which many of today's children could greatly benefit, the minister might also learn to enjoy some of the latest children's music—and it is being produced at an alarming rate. Much of it will clearly not pass the test of time, but much of it is very good, and this is largely due to the fact that children enjoy singing it!

Dramatic presentations are always valuable, both for the congregation and the performers, if they are well prepared and carefully presented. But not all churches are suitable for presentations by children. To have a dramatic offering which can be neither seen or heard is a negative, and far too frequent, contribution to worship. Some simple stage blocks, if not available in the church, can usually be borrowed from a school, or amateur theatrical company, and they can make all the difference to a service, when a child's offering can make people smile as they leave if done well—or frown in frustration if it is done without sufficient preparation on the part of the adults.

Index

ABC, 116
Ablutions, 49, 74, 77, 78
Absolution, 28, 32, 61
Accession service, 3, 104
Acclamations, 50, 73, 92
ACTS, 123
Additional consecration, 51
Address, *see* preaching
Administration of communion,
  45, 75
Adoption, 80
Adult baptism, 82
Advent, 32, 61, 62, 102
Agapé, 58
AIDS, 77
Alms, 23, 65, 67, 70
Altar, 22, 53, 54, 83, 85, 107
Anointing, 85, 87
Ante-Communion, 63, 67, 108
Archdeacon, 9, 22, 46, 87
ASB, viii, 3, *et passim*
Ascension, 109
Ashes, 99
Ash Wednesday, 61, 106
Athanasian Creed, 36
Aumbry, 74, 107
Authorised Version, 26, 33

Bands, 28, 100
Banns, 23, 24, 88
Baptism, 3, 9, 14, 15, 24, 81ff., 109
BCP, viii, 3, *et passim*
Bell, 7
Benedicite, 32, 33
Benedictus, 63, 72
Bible, 29, 30, 59

Bible Society, 104
Biddings, 39, 66
Bishop, 4, 5, 6, 7, 9, 10, 22, 33, 45,
  46, 47, 82, 85, 86, 87, 88, 96, 97,
  98, 105, 107
Blessing, 43, 76, 77, 78, 81, 85, 89,
  97, 107
Bow, 72
Breaking of Bread, 71, 74
Broderers, 56
Burial, *see* Funeral

Calendar, 36
Candle, Paschal, 109
Candles, 19, 20, 55, 85
Canon Law, 1
Cantate Domino, 32
Canticles, 29, 30, 32f., 63
Carols, 104
Cassock, 28
Centre of Worship, Parish, 7
Ceremonial, ix, 51
Chancellor, 17
Children, 69, 121, 122
Children's Society, 103, 106
Choir, 20, 59
Chrism, 97
Christian name, 81, 85, 86f.
Christingle, 102
Christmas, 62, 104
  tree, 103
Churching, 80
Churchmanship, ix
Churchwardens, 22, 27, 56, 87
Churchyard, 24
Ciborium, 70, 71

Collation, 4, 87
Collects, 36ff., 40, 49, 60, 62
Commandments, *see* Ten
    Commandments
Comfortable Words, 35, 68
Common cup, 77
Commons, 36
Communicant numbers, 23, 70
    status, 46
Communion, *see* Holy
    Communion
    of sick, 93
Compline, 44
Confession, 31, 61, 67
Confirmation, 3, 9, 24, 46, 82, 85,
    86, 121
Consecrated ground, 98
Consecration, 4, 45, 49, 50
Convocation, 2
Cope, 28, 90
Copyright, 25
Coroner, 98
Corpus Christi, 37, 73
Covenant service, 104
Credence, 19, 20, 55, 59, 77
Creed, 29, 35, 41, 49, 60, 65
Cremation, 24, 99
Crib, 103
Crossbearer, 22

DAC, 6, 17, 54
Daughter Church, 5
Deacon, x, 44, 45, 78, 81, 89, 98
Deaconess, 45, 81, 98
Decalogue, *see* Ten
    Commandments
Dedication, 4
Deliverance, 86
Deus Misereatur, 32
Dismissal, 78
Dispensation, 6
Distribution of elements, 45
Divorce, 88, 89
Drama, 53, 123

Easter, 4, 62, 105, 109
    anthems, 32
    garden, 109
Ecumenism, 27, 28, 60, 108
Elevation, 52, 72
Entry, 21
Epiphany, 103
Epistle, 46, 63
Eucharist, *see* Holy Communion
Eucharistic prayers, 8, 50f., 71
Evangelistic services, 4, 43, 116,
    121
Evening Prayer, Evensong, 6, 7,
    20, 23, ch. 4 *passim*, 63, 80, 83,
    122
Ewer, 19, 84, 85
Exhortations, 62
Exorcism, 96
Experiment, 16
Extempore prayer, 38f., 66, 67

Facing the people, 17, 54
Faculty, 17, 54
Fasting, 82
Family services, 4, ch. 10 *passim*
Font, 83
Footwashing, 107
Footwear, 19
Funeral, 3, 9, 24, 79, 98ff., 109

Garden, Easter, 109
General Synod, 1, 2, 4, 25, 33, 87,
    88
Genuflexion, 52, 72
Gifts, 69
Giving away the bride, 91
Gloria in Excelsis, 32, 49, 58, 60,
    63
Glory and Honour, 33
Godparents, 81, 84
Gospel, 46, 49, 63
    procession, 53
Grace, 40, 41, 63

Gradual, 63, 64
Great and Wonderful, 33
Guest services, 43

Harvest, 58, 110
Healing services, 4, 43, 94ff.
Holy Communion, 5, 6, 7, 14, 20,
   22, 30, 33, 39, chs 5 and 6
   passim, 80, 83, 100, 101, 108,
   120
Holy Saturday, 108
Holy Week, 4, 105ff.
Hospital services, 2, 24, 82
House blessing, 97
Humble Access, 49, 68
Hygiene, 77
Hymn, 21, 22, 25, 60, 63, 78, 80,
   90, 101, 123

Incumbent, 4, 5, 7, 9, 10, 11, 24,
   27, 46
Industrial Harvest Festival, 110
Institution and Induction, 4, 87
Intercessions, 16, 29, 30, 38, 49,
   53, 66, 108
Interim Rite, 49
Intinction, 73, 93
Introit, 60, 63
Invitation, 28, 31, 74

Jubilate Deo, 32

Kyrie litany, 117
Kyries, 58, 60

Law, ch. 1 *passim*
Lay chairman, 9
lay person, 32, 46, 81
Lectionary, 30, 31, 33, 35, 62
Lent, 4, 32, 61, 105ff.

Lessons, 33, 49, 52, 62
Licensing, 4, 5, 87
Linen, 56
Litany, 7, 29, 30, 41, 117
Liturgical Commission, vii, 4, 88
   preaching, 64
Liturgy of Word (or Sacrament),
   see Ministry
Local Ecumenical Project, 28, 46
Lord's Prayer, 29, 61, 63, 74, 81

Magnificat, 104
Manual acts, 51, 72
Marriage, 3, 4, 6, 9, 24, 88ff.
Mattins, *see* Morning Prayer
Maundy Thursday, 73, 85, 97, 107
Memorial services, 101
Minister, 27
Ministry of Sacrament, 16, 20, 48,
   54, 58, 69ff., 121
Ministry of Word, 16, 20, 53, 58,
   62ff., 108, 121
Missionary work, 37
Mission services, 4
Morning Prayer, 6, 7, 20, 23, ch. 4
   passim, 63, 80, 83
Music, ix, 16, 19

New Year, 104
Nine lessons, service of, 104, 108
North side, 54
Notices, 22, 65
Nullity, 88

Oblation, prayer of, 50
Oblations, 67
Occasional Offices, 9, 10, ch. 7
   passim
Offertory, 19, 65, 70
Offices, daily, *see* Evening Prayer,
   Morning Prayer
O Gladsome Light, 32

Oil, 85, 107
Orders of service, 115
Ordinary, 3, 4, 5, 41
Our Father, *see* Lord's Prayer

Palm Sunday, 62, 106
Parish Centre of Worship, 7
Parish church, 5, 6
Parish priest, *see* incumbent
Paschal candle, 85, 109
Passion readings, 63, 106, 107
PCC, viii, 6, 7, 8, 10, 11, 12, 16, 17, 28, 33, 46, 47, 56
Peace, 68
Penitence, 60, 67
Pentecost, 62
Post-communion, 78
Posture, 72, 76
Praetermissions, 37
Prayer and Praise, 4, 43
Prayer Book (Versions of the Bible) Measure, *see* Versions
Preacher, 23
Preaching, sermon, 7, 28, 29, 30, 42, 49, 64, 80, 83, 90
Preface, 49, 73
Preparation, the, 31, 55, 59, 69
Priest, 32, 45, 81, 89, 98
Procession, 19, 21, 63, 64
Proof-reading, 115
Propers, 36, 73, 92
Psalms, psalter, 30, 33, 63
Psychic disturbances, 96
Purificator, 77, 84, 85

Queen's accession, 3, 104
Queen, collect for, 61
Quicunque vult, 36
Quinquagesima, 62

Reader, x, 27, 34, 44

Reception into the Church of England, 87
Red Letter Days, 36, 38
Registers, 23f., 81, 87, 90, 92
Registrar, 6, 24, 98
Remembrance Sunday, 4, 110
Renewal of Vows, 109
Requiem, 96
Reserved Sacrament, 74, 93, 108
Reverencing the altar, 22
Rites, A and B, 48f.
Rogation, 109
Rota of services, 15
Rules to Order the Service, 37
Rural Dean, 9, 27, 28, 86

Sacristan, 55
Saints' Days, 36f.
Sanctus, 72
Saviour of the World, 32
Scarf, 28
School services, 2
Scripture, *see* Bible
Sentences, 28, 31
Series 1–3, 3, 28, 49, 72, 82, 89, 98
Sermon, *see* Preaching
Servers, 54
Seven Words, 108
Sexist language, 8
Shortened Services Act, 3, 28
Shrove Tuesday, 62
Sick, 3, 6, 74, 82, 93ff.
Sign of the Cross, 85, 98
Silence, 31, 34
Song of Creation, 33
Special licence, 6
Sponsors, *see* Godparents
Stage management, 16, 51f.
State Prayers, 39, 105
Stewardship, 58
Stole, 90, 100
Stripping the altars, 107
'Substantial importance', 8

Summary of the Law, 61, 68
Sunday School, 4, 14
Supplementary consecration, 51
Surplice, 28, 90, 100
Sursum Corda, 72

Table, holy, *see* Altar
Talking, 19
Te Deum, 29, 63, 105
Ten Commandments, 61, 68
Thanksgiving, 49, 50, 67, 71
    after birth, 80
Thanksgivings, 67
Three Hours' Devotion, 107
Trinity Sunday, 73

Unconsecrated ground, 98
Unction, 95, 97
Unity, 37

Variations, 2

Veneration of the Cross, 108
Venite, 29, 32, 60, 63
Verger, 22, 93
Versicles and responses, 29, 42, 67
Versions of the Bible, 33, 63
Vessels, sacred, 19, 20, 53, 55, 59
Vestry, 20
    prayer, 21, 59, 78
Vesture, vestments, ix, 28, 47, 55
Vigil, 109
Visitation of the Sick, 93
Visitations, 87
Vows, renewal of, 109

Wafer bread, 71
Watch, 107
Water, holy, 97
Wedding, *see* Marriage
Wine, 71
Worship and Doctrine Measure,
    1, 11